Salvation LIFE BOOKS

Helping people grow through spiritual formation books and experiences informed by the Wesleyan tradition.

SalvationLife.com/books

40 Days of Preparing the Soul for Easter

Follow

Daniel Ethan Harris

SalvationLife Books
www.salvationlife.com/books
E-mail: daniel@salvationlife.com

Copyright © 2013 Daniel Ethan Harris

All rights reserved. No part of this book may be reproduced in any form without written permission from SalvationLife Books.

ISBN-10: 0615857620
ISBN-13: 978-0615857626

Cover design: Roy Migabon: roymigabon.weebly.com
Cover image: Paul Prescott/Shutterstock

When noted as "NIV," scripture quotations are from THE HOLY BIBLE, NEW INTERNATIONAL VERSION®, NIV® Copyright © 1973, 1978, 1984, 2011 by Biblica, Inc.® Used by permission. All rights reserved worldwide.

Unless otherwise noted, prayers are from *The Book of Common Prayer of the Episcopal Church*, 1979 Edition, Public Domain.

Excerpt from *Praying in the Wesleyan Spirit: 52 Prayers for Today* by Paul Chilcote. Copyright ©2001 by Paul Chilcote. Used by permission of Upper Room Books. www.books.upperroom.org

For Kara,
my greatest encourager,
my best friend,
by whose side I always want to be
as we follow Jesus together.

Contents

Preface	9
Week 1: What Lent Is and What Lent Isn't	11
Week 2: Deny Yourself, Take Up Your Cross, and Follow Me	20
Week 3: When You Give	39
Week 4: When You Pray	57
Week 5: When You Fast	77
Week 6: A Road Map for Returning to God	99
Week 7: Holy Week	121
Easter: Because of the Resurrection	146
Notes	149

Preface

Whether or not you are from a church tradition that observes the season of Lent, if you are like me, there has been some year of your life when Easter came and went with minimal impact on you. Sometimes, within twenty-four hours after waking up on Easter Sunday, the only sign that the day ever came might be the leftover candy in the kids' baskets. Perhaps, if you are like me, that not only describes some past year of your life, but most years of your life.

Yet if it is indeed true that there was once an unofficial rabbi in ancient Israel who caused quite a stir before being executed by crucifixion and then later walked out of his own tomb, and I am one who–by using the name "Christian"–claims to give him the highest allegiance and devotion of every part of my life, Easter's impact on me should last longer than the candy.

The daily readings and prayers in this book will help you be more prepared for Easter this year. Built on the long-standing tradition of many Christians around the world of preparing for Easter through the forty days of Lent, this book takes you on a journey from Ash Wednesday to Easter Sunday, digging into different themes of Lent during each week.

You will notice that there are readings and prayers for each day of the week except Sundays. That is because, traditionally, Christians have not considered Sundays part of Lent in order to preserve every Sunday as a celebration of Jesus' resurrection (a mini-Easter). I think that's wise; not only can we be better prepared for Easter by observing Lent, but we can also better celebrate on that one Sunday of the year if we have practiced celebrating it on the other fifty-one.

This book originated as a series of daily Lenten emails I was asked to create for my church, First United Methodist of Midland, Texas. I am deeply grateful for that invitation from my pastor, Dr. Tim Walker, and for his encouragement as well as that of many others within our congregation. I love my church.

Putting a project like this together well requires a team a people. I am particularly thankful for the help of Ryan Bash, Tim Holeman, Laura Wheeler, and Christy Swaringen. Roy Migabon is a talented professional artist whose work on the covers for this project and *Live Prayerfully* has helped turn these ideas into reality.

And I couldn't write without my family. My wife, Kara's, contribution to anything I do is inestimable. She is the first person whose feedback I want, she gives me space to continue to indulge in this newfound writing habit, and she has a gift for making everything around her more enjoyable–including this book. Ethan and Mia bring me more joy than I ever expected. I hope that they both always know me as one who follows the Messiah, and that they will know the deep goodness of doing so as well.

Day 1: Ash Wednesday

It's Lent, Not Lint

I remember a time as a teenager when my youth pastor liked to joke about things he had given up for Lent. For example, if someone suggested that he wash his car or mow his lawn, his response would be, "I can't. I gave it up for Lent."

I laughed every time I heard him make one of those jokes, even though it turned out that I really didn't get his punch line. Since I had no idea what the church season of Lent was, I thought that he was saying he had given up things for "lint." Like many things kids that age find humorous, I now realize that wouldn't have made any sense, but still my middle-school brain thought it was funny. I imagined my youth pastor sitting at home with his precious collection of lint rolled into a large ball, with his dirty car and tall weeds in the yard.

Thankfully, the church's season of Lent is something much more meaningful than that. Lent is about finding ways to return to God with our whole hearts. The things we do today, Ash Wednesday, are designed to give us concrete ways of beginning again our return to God. We pray; we read scripture, including the great prayer of repentance from Psalm 51; we allow our pastors to place ashes in the sign of a cross on our foreheads to remind us that our lives in this age are fleeting, to mark us as the people of the crucified Messiah, and to remember that we are utterly dependent on the life that God gives us as a gift both today and forever. We invite God to search us and help us to see our sin, while trusting that he is full of compassion and mercy, and then we consider the ways that we can best arrange these lives he has given us around the invitation to come and adore him.

A Prayer for Ash Wednesday:

O God,
maker of every thing and judge of all that you have made,
from the dust of the earth you have formed us
and from the dust of death you would raise us up.
By the redemptive power of the cross,
create in us clean hearts
and put within us a new spirit,
that we may repent of our sins
and lead lives worthy of your calling;
through Jesus Christ our Lord. Amen.[1]

Day 2: Thursday

Lent's Invitation

As I shared yesterday, for years I had no idea what Lent really is. Even after I learned that Lent has been an important part of our habits in the church for centuries, I still had very little understanding of why we do things the way we do. As has often been the case for me, I was pleasantly surprised to find something very helpful right within my own tradition. The following "Invitation to Observance of Lenten Discipline" [perhaps could use a more exciting title, but] is part of the United Methodist liturgy for Ash Wednesday and gives a helpful explanation of what Lent is and an invitation to participate:

Dear brothers and sisters in Christ:

the early Christians observed with great devotion the days of our Lord's passion and resurrection, and it became the custom of the Church that before the Easter celebration there should be a forty-day season of spiritual preparation.

During this season converts to the faith were prepared for Holy Baptism. It was also a time when persons who had committed serious sins and had separated themselves from the community of faith were reconciled by penitence and forgiveness, and restored to participation in the life of the Church. In this way the whole congregation was reminded of the mercy and forgiveness proclaimed in the gospel of Jesus Christ and the need we all have to renew our faith.

I invite you, therefore, in the name of the Church, to observe a holy Lent: by self-examination and repentance; by prayer, fasting, and self-denial; and by reading and meditating upon God's Holy Word....[2]

I hope that, if you sense any kind of invitation for the kind of Lent described above to characterize your days between now and Easter, that you can take a moment now in prayer and dedicate these weeks of your life to God and his work of grace in you.

A Prayer for the Day:
Heavenly Father, in you we live and move and have our being: We humbly pray you so to guide and govern us by your Holy Spirit, that in all the cares and occupations of our life we may not forget you, but may remember that we are ever walking in your sight; through Jesus Christ our Lord. Amen.

A Prayer for the Week:
Almighty God, whose blessed Son was led by the Spirit to be tempted by Satan; Come quickly to help us who are assaulted by many temptations; and, as you know the weaknesses of each of us, let each one find you mighty to save; through Jesus Christ your Son our Lord, who lives and reigns with you and the Holy Spirit, one God, now and for ever. Amen.

Day 3: Friday

A Bad Idea for Lent and a Really Good One

Several years ago, I had a friend who gave up breath mints for Lent. The guy had a good heart, but please–if you love God and those around you–don't consider following his example this year. Of all the possible things God might desire for you during the coming weeks, I'm quite sure that there is no good connection between holiness and halitosis.

Hopefully it isn't breath mints, but is there something else you've thought about giving up as a way of observing Lent? Maybe you've known others who have given things up along the lines of my friend and his unfortunate forty-day abstinence from fresh breath, so you've decided that doing so isn't for you.

Giving something up or taking on a practice during these weeks can be helpful, but any decision to do so needs to be set in the right context in order for it to be beneficial. Sometimes, we tend to think that if there's anything we enjoy, we would be really spiritual if we decided to abstain from it during Lent. So, we end up saying no to things like chocolate (or breath mints) in order to really feel like we're making a sacrifice for God.

Being intentional about our practices during these weeks of Lent is an excellent idea, but we should be careful not to confuse the means (our spiritual practices) with the end (opening our lives to God) as we think about the things we're giving up or the things we're taking on. Ruth Haley Barton states the point of our Lenten practices succinctly by framing them with the question:

How will I find ways to return to God with all my heart?[3]

I hope that you can let that question simmer in your mind through the remainder of this week. As each of us does so, we can trust that God will lead us.

A Prayer for the Day:
Almighty God, whose most dear Son went not up to joy but first he suffered pain, and entered not into glory before he was crucified: Mercifully grant that we, walking in the way of the cross, may find it none other than the way of life and peace; through Jesus Christ our Lord. Amen.

A Prayer for the Week:
Almighty God, whose blessed Son was led by the Spirit to be tempted by Satan; Come quickly to help us who are assaulted by many temptations; and, as you know the weaknesses of each of us, let each one find you mighty to save; through Jesus Christ your Son our Lord, who lives and reigns with you and the Holy Spirit, one God, now and for ever. Amen.

Day 4: Saturday

What You Might Need Most

Throughout this first week of Lent, I have tried to help us set the context for practices that can help us return to God with all our hearts in the coming weeks. In this final introductory reflection, I want to propose a type of practice which may seem unusual, but of which I believe many of us are in desperate need. What if, this Lent, you set a spiritual goal of getting enough rest?

Many of us have become accustomed to being so tired that we've forgotten what it feels like to be fully rested. This is often tied to a misconception, thinking that our bodies are disconnected from our spiritual lives. That idea is very prevalent among Christians, but–wherever it comes from–it doesn't come from the Bible.

Throughout the Old and New Testaments, God continually emphasized the importance of rest in the lives of his people. Rest is a concrete way that we learn to trust God and to express our dependence upon him. This has primarily been practiced through the centuries as God's people have observed a Sabbath day each week to rest from our work, worship God for his steadfast love toward us, and engage in activities that delight and refresh us. As one of my favorite authors, James Bryan Smith, says, we can't do anything worthwhile spiritually if we're exhausted.[4]

So, here is a brief list of things you might consider if setting a goal of getting enough rest seems inviting to you this Lent:

- If you tend to stay up too late, set three bedtimes for yourself: an ideal bedtime, an okay bedtime, and an "anything later than this is unacceptable" bedtime. As you go to rest each night, think of it as a spiritual practice, helping you to express your trust in God that he can take care of the things that were not accomplished in the day.
- Determine that, this Lent, you won't stay late at work.
- Set aside a 24-hour period each week this Lent during which your goal is not to be distracted, but to pay attention to those who are with you. You might start this 24 hours in the evening, as you share a slow meal with family or friends. You'll probably find it very helpful (though difficult) to turn off your cell phone. Take a break from e-mail and internet, even all media if possible. Go to bed at a good time that evening, being free of the usual distractions. Either verbally or through writing, affirm to someone their importance in your life.
- Another way we can rest is to intentionally take a break from thinking about things we don't have, and, instead, give thanks to God for all of the ways that he has provided for us so faithfully. This might mean cutting back on shopping and increasing your generosity. Or perhaps you might simply want to choose to live with the mindset this Lent: "I have enough." As we do so over time, we find that our gratitude and our ability to trust God with our needs increases.

Day 4: Saturday

A Prayer for the Day:

Almighty God, who after the creation of the world rested from all your works and sanctified a day of rest for all your creatures: Grant that we, putting away all earthly anxieties, may be duly prepared for the service of your sanctuary, and that our rest here upon earth may be a preparation for the eternal rest promised to your people in heaven; through Jesus Christ our Lord. Amen.

A Prayer for the Week:

Almighty God, whose blessed Son was led by the Spirit to be tempted by Satan; Come quickly to help us who are assaulted by many temptations; and, as you know the weaknesses of each of us, let each one find you mighty to save; through Jesus Christ your Son our Lord, who lives and reigns with you and the Holy Spirit, one God, now and for ever. Amen.

Day 5: Monday

Jesus' Most Repeated Instruction

It's surprising how many of the famous things Jesus said don't appear in all four of the gospels (Matthew, Mark, Luke, and John). For example, statements such as "do not judge" and the Golden Rule are only in Matthew and Luke. "Seek first the kingdom of God" is unique to Matthew. "Father, forgive them, for they know not what they do" is only found in Luke. John's account is the only place where Jesus says, "I am the way, the truth, and the life."

An important part of letting the message of the scriptures sink deeply into us is to learn to pay attention to the distinct ways in which each writer of scripture told their part of the story, particularly in the gospels. The flip side of that method, though, is that the things that do appear in all four of the gospels really deserve our attention. For example, the only miracle that Jesus performed which is recounted by all four gospel writers is Jesus' feeding of the five thousand. Apparently they all saw that event as central enough to Jesus' story that each of them had to include it.

Along these lines, there is one of Jesus' teachings that is included in the gospels more often than any other. Each of the gospel writers makes it part of their narrative, and Matthew and Luke each include it twice.

So what is the statement of Jesus which Matthew, Mark, Luke, and John saw as important enough to repeat to their readers a total of six times?

"Whoever wants to save their life will lose it, but whoever loses their life for me will find it."[5]

Apparently, this is a phrase that sank deeply into virtually every follower of Jesus in those first generations of disciples. They saw him give up his own life, both in the way that he lived for others and ultimately in his death. When they became his followers and took on his way of life, this was one of the key ways of describing what that life meant for them.

In this week's readings, we'll explore this teaching of Jesus and its importance for us this Lent. In doing so, we will look at the statement often connected with it in those gospel stories: "Whoever wants to be my disciple must deny themselves, take up their cross and follow me."[6]

A Prayer for the Day:
O God, the King eternal, whose light divides the day from the night and turns the shadow of death into the morning: Drive far from us all wrong desires, incline our hearts to keep your law, and guide our feet into the way of peace; that, having done your will with cheerfulness while it was day, we may, when night comes, rejoice to give you thanks; through Jesus Christ our Lord. Amen.

A Prayer for the Week:
O God, whose glory it is always to have mercy: Be gracious to all who have gone astray from your ways, and bring them again with penitent hearts and steadfast faith to embrace and hold fast the unchangeable truth of your Word, Jesus Christ your Son; who with you and the Holy Spirit lives and reigns, one God, for ever and ever. Amen.

Day 6: Tuesday

Deny Yourself
(But Not Like This)

Christians have done some well-intentioned but very silly things through the centuries in our efforts to do what Jesus said. Particularly in trying to apply Jesus' statement that anyone who wants to be his disciple must deny themselves, take up their cross and follow him, some percentage of our track record could be categorized as well-meaning adventures in missing the point.

While my wife and I lived as missionaries in Guatemala, we visited a cathedral which was hundreds of years old, part of which was dedicated as a shrine to a local saint, Hermano Pedro. It appears that Pedro was certainly a good guy who did a lot of good things, but one of the relics in the museum dedicated to his memory stood out as a classic misguided example of self-denial in the name of Jesus: there, preserved since the mid 1600's, was a pair of Hermano Pedro's burlap underwear which he would wear as a method of self-denial.

I grew up on a pecan farm, where I sometimes had the job of moving 100-pound burlap sacks of pecans, and that limited experience with the rough, irritating burlap was enough to convince me that Pedro's method wasn't for me. Plus, with all due respect to Pedro, I'm pretty confident that burlap undies wasn't what Jesus had in mind when he issued his call to discipleship.

However, even if some throughout Christian history have erred on the burlap underwear side of things, perhaps it's much more common for us today to make the opposite mistake and not take self-denial seriously enough in our lives with God. In fact, the founder Methodism, John Wesley, claimed that whenever any of us is not growing in God's grace, whenever we are anything less than Christ's fully-devoted disciples, it is always due to a lack of self-denial.[7]

As we follow Jesus, the crucified and risen Messiah, we will inevitably find that once we have decided to deny ourselves, eventually a cross awaits us. Over the next couple of days, we will explore what "take up your cross" meant to Jesus' original disciples when he said it, then what it might mean to us as his disciples today.

To help us take some steps along this road of self-denial throughout this year's season of Lent, perhaps questions like this might begin to point us in a helpful direction:
- How do I handle it when I don't get my way?
- Do I spend much mental effort on my own reputation?
- Which do I tend to value more: being right or being Christlike?
- Do I have any habits which help me intentionally practice self-control?

Follow

A Prayer for the Day:
O God, the author of peace and lover of concord, to know you is eternal life and to serve you is perfect freedom: Defend us, your humble servants, in all assaults of our enemies; that we, surely trusting in your defense, may not fear the power of any adversaries; through the might of Jesus Christ our Lord. Amen.

A Prayer for the Week:
O God, whose glory it is always to have mercy: Be gracious to all who have gone astray from your ways, and bring them again with penitent hearts and steadfast faith to embrace and hold fast the unchangeable truth of your Word, Jesus Christ your Son; who with you and the Holy Spirit lives and reigns, one God, for ever and ever. Amen.

Day 7: Wednesday

Take Up Your Cross: What it Meant to Them

There once was a popular political figure who, when it seemed like his reputation with the public was at an amazingly high level, gathered his closest group of associates in order to gauge their thoughts on his future. He asked them, "What is the public's opinion of my abilities?"

These people he trusted responded by naming other successful political figures from history to whom he was often being compared in the press. This was a good sign. It meant the hopes and trust of the public in him were high. So, looking at the faces of his deeply trusted coworkers and friends, he asked the question he'd been waiting to ask them ever since they entered the political arena together: "And what about you? What do you think of my chances?"

The most powerful among them immediately spoke up and said, "You are destined to be the next leader of this nation."

"Let's do it," the esteemed leader responded decisively. "But keep it to yourselves for now. I already have our strategy planned: I will do things that will cause everyone currently in power to reject me. I will be humiliated in the worst ways possible. I will challenge their power so fundamentally that charges of treason likely await me—and the death penalty will almost certainly follow."

The one who (just minutes before) had affirmed the leader's destiny then cried out, "You're out of your mind!"

"You, get out of my way, along with your accusations," the leader responded sharply. "You're only seeing things from your own very limited perspective."

Then he said loudly to his associates and anyone else within earshot,

> *Anyone who intends to come with me has to let me lead. You're not in the driver's seat; I am. Don't run from suffering; embrace it. Follow me and I'll show you how. Self-help is no help at all. Self-sacrifice is the way, my way, to saving yourself, your true self. What good would it do to get everything you want and lose you, the real you? What could you ever trade your soul for?*[8]

I hope this story rings some bells for you. Perhaps you are able to recognize it as an adaptation of a conversation between Jesus and his disciples (see Mark 8:27-38), though—if you're like me—you may have heard those passages for years without ever having been able to see the political (kingdom) aspects of what Jesus said and did.

When we read Peter saying, "You are the Messiah," we often interpret that as Peter recognizing Jesus as the second person of the Trinity, but that isn't what Peter meant by it, nor how the other disciples would have understood what he said. He was saying, in effect, "You are the one, anointed by God and foretold by the prophets, who will be able to lead us out of this mess."

The disciples were beginning to understand a small part of what Jesus' work was about, then seizing on that degree of understanding, Jesus told them what was about to happen: that he would suffer, die, and rise again. To his disciples, this was inconceivable if he really was who Peter had just described. As N.T. Wright points out, this is like a captain of a football team telling his squad that in the second half of the game he intended to let the opposing team score ten consecutive touchdowns. "Jesus seemed to be saying he was going to lose. Worse, he was inviting them to come and lose alongside him."[9]

None of the spiritual meaning we usually attach today to "deny yourself, take up your cross, and follow me" existed for Peter and the other disciples that night. Those were dangerous, incomprehensible, impossible to swallow words. Now that they recognized Jesus as the Messiah, every idea they had of what the Messiah should do was about to be shattered. And he was asking them to take the same path.

Does he ask anything different of you?

Follow

A Prayer for the Day:
Lord God, almighty and everlasting Father, you have brought us in safety to this new day: Preserve us with your mighty power, that we may not fall into sin, nor be overcome by adversity; and in all we do, direct us to the fulfilling of your purpose; through Jesus Christ our Lord. Amen.

A Prayer for the Week:
O God, whose glory it is always to have mercy: Be gracious to all who have gone astray from your ways, and bring them again with penitent hearts and steadfast faith to embrace and hold fast the unchangeable truth of your Word, Jesus Christ your Son; who with you and the Holy Spirit lives and reigns, one God, for ever and ever. Amen.

Day 8: Thursday

Take Up Your Cross: What it Means to Us

My father-in-law, a life-long devoted Christian, asked me a question I could tell he had wrestled with for some time: "What does it mean for me to take up my cross?"

Here was a phrase which he and I had both heard our entire lives as Christians, but which–when we're honest–is difficult for most of us to attach any practical meaning to in the way we live our day-to-day lives. I gave my best stumbling attempt to answer him, though I didn't feel like my effort at doing so was very helpful. It was a great question and is worth wrestling with.

The large majority of people who will ever read this face no immediate danger to their lives as a result of calling themselves followers of Jesus. There are millions of Christians around the world for whom that is not the case and to whom this statement of Jesus has a much more straightforward meaning: "Whoever wants to be my disciple must deny themselves and take up their cross and follow me. For whoever wants to save their life will lose it, but whoever loses their life for me and for the gospel will save it."

But what about the rest of us? How, *really*, are Christians in the 21st century supposed to take up our crosses and follow an ancient Jewish rabbi?

The things we commonly identify as our "cross to bear" are almost comical when held up next to what Jesus' statement would have meant to its original audience. Jesus meant that he was going toward his death and anyone who wanted to follow him would likely be facing theirs as well; we mean things like someone in our office annoys us or that we don't get our way about something. *The Free Dictionary* defines the phrase, "cross to bear/cross to carry" as, "an unpleasant situation or responsibility that you must accept because you cannot change it."[10] That's a huge reduction from the journey that Jesus intentionally took toward his death in Jerusalem. The gospels make it pretty clear that Jesus was trying to use stronger language than saying, "If anyone wants to be my disciple, they might have to accept something that's unpleasant."

But if that isn't the meaning of the phrase for us today, what is?

Perhaps there are two levels on which we can think about this:

First, the meaning closest to that which the disciples would have understood when they were with him on that night: Regardless of our time and culture, *truly following Jesus involves risk*. The call to take up our cross and follow the crucified and risen Messiah is more risky than dealing with an unpleasant situation or making a few minor adjustments to our ordinary lives. No, this is an invitation to a risky life in God's kingdom, which–until Jesus' reign is the only one left–will always have its points of costly conflict with the powers and ways of the world. As one of my modern-day heroes, Gary Haugen (president and CEO of International Justice Mission), says,

"Here is one choice that our Father wants us to understand as Christians–and I believe this is the choice of our age: Do we want to be brave or be safe? Gently, lovingly, our heavenly Father wants us to know that we simply can't be both."[11]

If we are in any way to let the original meaning of Jesus' statement shape its meaning for us today, we have to recognize that "Jesus is not leading us on a pleasant afternoon hike, but on a walk into danger and risk."[12] Perhaps your risk includes becoming involved with work like that of International Justice Mission. Perhaps it means standing up against wrongdoing in your own community. Or perhaps you already have another idea of how following Jesus could lead you into things that are not always safe and comfortable, but still important extensions of God's kingdom-work on earth.

The second level is a bit more metaphorical, but still consistent with the message of the scriptures. Paul says that sin was condemned in Jesus' flesh when he was crucified. When we follow him to our own crosses, sin will be dealt with in our bodies as well. This is a big subject, and an essential one for us to understand if we are to make sense of how the things we do each and every day relate to our participation in Christ's kingdom right now.

Even though we cannot address all of the issues here, we can begin with the understanding that everything we do in our spiritual lives is done in our bodies, and that any habits–whether holy or sinful–are always embodied habits. Therefore, in the traditional readings for Ash

Wednesday, when Jesus says, "When you give... When you pray... When you fast...," these are all things we do in our bodies in order to replace (actually the Bible says, to *kill off*) sinful habits by putting in place other routines more conducive to God's life in us. When we deny ourselves, take up our crosses, and follow him, we resubmit any part of us that is unlike Jesus to be killed off so that his grace can continue its life-giving work in us.

A Prayer for the Day:

Heavenly Father, in you we live and move and have our being: We humbly pray you so to guide and govern us by your Holy Spirit, that in all the cares and occupations of our life we may not forget you, but may remember that we are ever walking in your sight; through Jesus Christ our Lord. Amen.

A Prayer for the Week:

O God, whose glory it is always to have mercy: Be gracious to all who have gone astray from your ways, and bring them again with penitent hearts and steadfast faith to embrace and hold fast the unchangeable truth of your Word, Jesus Christ your Son; who with you and the Holy Spirit lives and reigns, one God, for ever and ever. Amen.

Day 9: Friday

Your Followership Skills

As much as the world around us, especially in the culture where I live, emphasizes the need for leadership and the development of our leadership skills, Lent is an annual reminder to us that–at least during these days each year–our focus is rightly put on our abilities and skills as *followers*. Though we are quick to turn everything into a call to leadership, the statement from Jesus we've been looking at this week says nothing about growing the influence we have over others and everything about growing the influence that this Messiah-en-route-to-his-death has over us: *"Whoever wants to be my disciple must deny themselves and take up their cross and follow me. For whoever wants to save their life will lose it, but whoever loses their life for me and for the gospel will save it."*

Lent invites us to lay aside the urge to continue measuring ourselves by our competencies as leaders and focus instead, very honestly, on our competencies as followers of Jesus. Are we developing the abilities that will be required over the long haul in this daily journey of denying ourselves, taking up our crosses and following our king? Here are three essential areas in which we would be wise to continually develop our followership[13]:

- **Our Minds:** How well do we know the story of this ancient Jew whom we claim to be following? I don't see how it can be possible to follow someone well while knowing very little about them. So how well do we know the stories of Jesus contained in the books of Matthew, Mark, Luke and John?

  Once we try to learn them well, we will surely recognize that we need some help in understanding some of them, which will lead us to a second set of stories we need to learn well: those stories that shaped the thinking of our Leader himself, the stories of God, Israel, and the world in the Old Testament.

  If we desire to follow Jesus well, during this Lent and the rest of our lives, we must fill our minds with these stories, constantly letting them sink in more deeply.

- **Our Habits:** Do the habits that we have make it *natural* for us to follow Jesus toward the cross, or do they only serve as obstacles in the way of any efforts we make at followership? The things we do either open us up to God's work in us, or they close us off to it.

- **Our Relationships:** Denying ourselves, taking up our crosses, and following Jesus are impossible alone. We pay attention to the importance of relationships in leadership, but it is underemphasized when it comes to our abilities to follow. Which relationships that you now have help you to follow Jesus well? Which ones tend to get you off track?

Day 9: Friday

A Prayer for the Day:
Almighty God, whose most dear Son went not up to joy but first he suffered pain, and entered not into glory before he was crucified: Mercifully grant that we, walking in the way of the cross, may find it none other than the way of life and peace; through Jesus Christ our Lord. Amen.

A Prayer for the Week:
O God, whose glory it is always to have mercy: Be gracious to all who have gone astray from your ways, and bring them again with penitent hearts and steadfast faith to embrace and hold fast the unchangeable truth of your Word, Jesus Christ your Son; who with you and the Holy Spirit lives and reigns, one God, for ever and ever. Amen.

Day 10: Saturday
Enchiladas, Steering Wheels, and Following Jesus to the Cross

Two things caught my attention at the beginning of Lent last year. The first one was an advertisement I saw above a gas pump while filling up my vehicle. It was an ad for a "Lenten Special" of three cheese enchiladas flanked by promotions on cigarettes and breakfast food. Promoted there, alongside the Marlboros and breakfast burritos, is–apparently–an opportunity to repent and hear a first-century Jewish rabbi's call to deny ourselves, take up our own crosses, and follow him as he walked the road into his own unjust death.

"Hey that sounds good. Oh, and let me grab a bag of Doritos to go with my three denying-myself cheese enchiladas. I think the man upstairs is pretty happy with me today! Maybe I'll even ask if they have any more sackcloth and ashes behind the counter when I get my cigarettes."[14]

The other attention-grabber was an article about churches offering drive-thru Ash Wednesday services. It is good for churches to begin to think beyond the way they've always done things. Much of the origin of my own Methodist heritage is based on how John Wesley was determined to preach in places that weren't normal. But still…

"From dust you came and to dust you will return. Repent and believe the gospel….Yes ma'am, that means changing the

entire course of your life….No ma'am, getting out of the car isn't required to do so…..Say, can you turn down that Lady Gaga on your radio so that you can hear me a little better? ….Okay, have a nice day [living exactly as you always have.]"

In their defense, someone has probably had an encounter with God right there in their car because of these churches doing this, and it wouldn't have happened otherwise. I'm sure that I don't know the whole story here, so I'm not offering criticism of these specific churches since I'm not there trying to figure out how to minister in their context.

But, in general, in what kind of training are we involving people when we encourage them to begin *Lent, of all times, without even bothering to get out of the car?* Or, to put it another way, what percentage of people receiving an imposition of ashes while continuing to sit behind their steering wheel would we honestly expect to continue, for the rest of their lives, down the road of being whole-hearted, full-throttle followers of Jesus? Again, there may be some example of someone to whom that has happened, for which I'm grateful. But is such a case a natural, predictable result of the way we do things with God, or are they just strange exceptions to the rule?

Lent is a time for house-cleaning our souls, so that when we come to Holy Week and Easter Sunday, we're prepared for the resurrection of the crucified Messiah to take more of its intended effect upon us. It's a time to pay attention to how dis-oriented we have become in the ways that we live our everyday lives and to find ways that we can re-orient ourselves to the one who said,

If any want to become my followers, let them deny themselves and take up their cross and follow me. For those who want to save their life will lose it, and those who lose

their life for my sake, and for the sake of the gospel, will save it. For what will it profit them to gain the whole world and forfeit their life? Indeed, what can they give in return for their life?

So if you and I got into the drive-thru line for our ashes to begin Lent this year, or picked up our Lenten enchiladas at the gas station, or whatever else it is that we may have done so far during this annual period of repentance and re-orientation, are the things that we're doing of the type that naturally help us, by God's grace, to become more likely and more able to follow Jesus with our own crosses in tow? Or are they things that just help us to feel religious while leaving the houses of our souls exactly as messy and disoriented as they were last Lent, and the one before, and the one before, etc.?

A Prayer for the Day:
Almighty God, who after the creation of the world rested from all your works and sanctified a day of rest for all your creatures: Grant that we, putting away all earthly anxieties, may be duly prepared for the service of your sanctuary, and that our rest here upon earth may be a preparation for the eternal rest promised to your people in heaven; through Jesus Christ our Lord. Amen.

A Prayer for the Week:
O God, whose glory it is always to have mercy: Be gracious to all who have gone astray from your ways, and bring them again with penitent hearts and steadfast faith to embrace and hold fast the unchangeable truth of your Word, Jesus Christ your Son; who with you and the Holy Spirit lives and reigns, one God, for ever and ever. Amen.

Day 11: Monday

When You Give...When You Pray...When You Fast

Every year, the first words of Jesus that we are given to read during Lent are the same.[15] They come from the Sermon on the Mount, which is likely the teaching of Jesus that has had more influence than any other in the two millennia between the time that he first spoke these words and today.

In this section of his sermon (Matthew 6:1-18–take a moment and read it now if possible), Jesus focused on spiritual practices, along with both helpful and unhelpful ways to observe them. This is why we begin each Lent with this passage. During the days leading up to Easter, we rightly increase our attention on our spiritual practices, because we can't return to God with all our hearts while continuing to do things as we always have. Yet Jesus' words indicate his adamance about two things:

First, these kinds of practices are so good that they will always be part of the lives of those who follow him in any real sense. Notice that Jesus did not say, "*If* you give...*if* you pray...*if* you fast," but "*when* you give...*when* you pray...*when* you fast..." His sermon assumes what was true in his day: that anyone committed to a devout life with God did these things then, and also that his followers in the future would continue to do them now.

Second, despite how good these practices are, it's possible to do them in ways that are harmful rather than helpful—both to us and those around us. We can give, pray, and fast in ways that open the channels for God's grace to work in our souls, or we can do them in ways that close those channels, but still leave us appearing very religiously devout in the eyes of others. Therefore—and this is Jesus' ultimate point in this passage—we should do these outward practices, but they miss the point without an inward openness to God.

For the next three weeks, we will dig in to this passage and these practices, focusing during the remainder of this week on "when you give," then next week on "when you pray," followed by "when you fast," seeking to find the most helpful ways that each of us can put them into practice in our lives today.

Day 11: Monday

A Prayer for the Day:

O God, the King eternal, whose light divides the day from the night and turns the shadow of death into the morning: Drive far from us all wrong desires, incline our hearts to keep your law, and guide our feet into the way of peace; that, having done your will with cheerfulness while it was day, we may, when night comes, rejoice to give you thanks; through Jesus Christ our Lord. Amen.

A Prayer for the Week:

Almighty God, you know that we have no power in ourselves to help ourselves: Keep us both outwardly in our bodies and inwardly in our souls, that we may be defended from all adversities which may happen to the body, and from all evil thoughts which may assault and hurt the soul; through Jesus Christ our Lord, who lives and reigns with you and the Holy Spirit, one God, for ever and ever. Amen.

Day 12: Tuesday

Don't Give to be Seen by Others

When I was in high school, I was part of a student club which occasionally did community service projects. Looking back now on my experience with that organization, apparently the point of its existence and of our participation in it was so that people could look at us and think, "O wow, look, they're part of that club that occasionally does community service projects."

I remember one project in particular, which we spent more time planning than any other. We had made preparations to give a group of single mothers a special day to themselves. We were going to provide childcare and arrangements had been made for the ladies to have an enjoyable day with manicures and other things that our female sponsor was sure these ladies would enjoy.

It was a good idea, but it fell apart for the worst of reasons. Providing those ladies with a restful and enjoyable day was a very secondary motivation for our group. The primary reason our club worked harder to organize that community service project than any other was the possibility of winning a statewide award for our school's chapter of the organization. The plan was in place: one person had a connection with someone from the newspaper, who would write up a story about our generous activities that day. Then our sponsor was going to make sure that the media's coverage of us got into the hands of people at the state level of our organization. We were sure that an award and recognition would follow.

The plan came to a crashing halt when, a few days before our project, the person from the newspaper let us know that something else had come up and they wouldn't be able to cover our [ridiculously self-centered] day of "service." The worst part of it all (for which I should probably get on my knees right now–decades later–and ask forgiveness) is that *we called the day off because the media wasn't going to be able to cover it.*

Lord, have mercy!

As a teenager, my peers and I (and our adult sponsor) obviously didn't know this teaching of Jesus very well:

Be careful not to practice your righteousness in front of others to be seen by them. If you do, you will have no reward from your Father in heaven. So when you give to the needy, do not announce it with trumpets, as the hypocrites do in the synagogues and on the streets, to be honored by others. Truly I tell you, they have received their reward in full. But when you give to the needy, do not let your left hand know what your right hand is doing, so that your giving may be in secret. Then your Father, who sees what is done in secret, will reward you.
(Matthew 6:1-4, NIV)

We cannot be both followers of Jesus and do good for others in order to be seen and get credit for it. Rather, followers of Jesus should give/do good for others so often–in every possible way and at every appropriate opportunity–that it becomes an ingrained habit, where we do good without even realizing what we've done.

That's the point about not letting "your left hand know what your right hand is doing."

It's like when we drive a certain route in a car so many times that eventually our body can virtually drive the route for us. Then sometimes we arrive at our destination and think, "How did I get here? Did I pass the store? Did I stop at that light?" (Okay, sometimes I do this. If no one else does, stay out of my way on the road.) From these words of Jesus, we are challenged to give to others often enough that the good things we do become routine, even to the point that we don't notice, and then it certainly won't matter whether others do or not.

A Prayer for the Day:
O God, the author of peace and lover of concord, to know you is eternal life and to serve you is perfect freedom: Defend us, your humble servants, in all assaults of our enemies; that we, surely trusting in your defense, may not fear the power of any adversaries; through the might of Jesus Christ our Lord. Amen.

A Prayer for the Week:
Almighty God, you know that we have no power in ourselves to help ourselves: Keep us both outwardly in our bodies and inwardly in our souls, that we may be defended from all adversities which may happen to the body, and from all evil thoughts which may assault and hurt the soul; through Jesus Christ our Lord, who lives and reigns with you and the Holy Spirit, one God, for ever and ever. Amen.

Day 13: Wednesday

Wesley's Guidelines for Giving to Others

One of my more peculiar hobbies is reading sermons from the 1700s by John Wesley. The positive side of this hobby is that his sermons were brilliant. The lives of Christians from any tradition would be deeply enriched by reading them. The negative side of this hobby is that his sermons were long and boring. Christians from any tradition would fall asleep while reading them. Apparently good jokes weren't seen as an essential part of sermon preparation in 18th century England.

From my perspective, the value of the sermons' brilliance outweighs the challenge of drudging through them, because of those times when I come across something that is exceptionally helpful.

This happened a couple of years ago as I was working my way through Wesley's series on Jesus' Sermon on the Mount. In the sermon [not so very creatively] titled, "Upon Our Lord's Sermon on the Mount, Discourse Three," Wesley responds to Jesus' statement, "Give to the one who asks you, and do not turn away from the one who wants to borrow from you" with three very simple, but very helpful guidelines. They apply just as well in our day as in his.

Follow

- *Carefully avoid being in debt to anyone.* Wesley makes the point that if we have debts, the things we give to help others are not our own to give, but they belong to someone else. Debt was a big problem in Wesley's day (his father, a priest, spent time in debtor's prison), and it is a huge problem for us today. Perhaps debt is more complex and sophisticated for us today than it was three hundred years ago, but the principle is still clear: We are freest to do good for others with our resources when we owe nothing to anyone.
- *Take care of your own household.* Wesley instructs us to not even consider things our own that are required for the physical and spiritual well-being of those in our own families. Caring for them is as much of a duty to God as anything else we do.
- *Then, give everything that remains, day by day and year by year for the good of others.* He also notes that we all have limitations on ourselves and our resources, making it impossible to address all of the world's needs. Therefore, we should first consider the needs of "the household of faith," our brothers and sisters in Christ, wherever they may be.

Certainly this plan, written so long ago, doesn't spell out every detail of how we should handle giving to others today. But it is a serious call to deny ourselves and follow Jesus through giving, and as we consider this week Jesus' words that we're given each Lent, "When you give...," we should reflect on how we can each best apply these three guidelines. (Perhaps a needed Lenten decision for some of us is to apply Wesley's guidelines in more detail, and an excellent plan for our day is contained in Dave Ramsey's "Seven Baby Steps" covered in detail in *Financial Peace University*.[16])

Day 13: Wednesday

A Prayer for the Day:

Lord God, almighty and everlasting Father, you have brought us in safety to this new day: Preserve us with your mighty power, that we may not fall into sin, nor be overcome by adversity; and in all we do, direct us to the fulfilling of your purpose; through Jesus Christ our Lord. Amen.

A Prayer for the Week:

Almighty God, you know that we have no power in ourselves to help ourselves: Keep us both outwardly in our bodies and inwardly in our souls, that we may be defended from all adversities which may happen to the body, and from all evil thoughts which may assault and hurt the soul; through Jesus Christ our Lord, who lives and reigns with you and the Holy Spirit, one God, for ever and ever. Amen.

Day 14: Thursday

The Difference We Can Make

One of my heroes was an old Texas oilman named Chester. Chester was a grandfather figure to me growing up, and he was one for whom giving was a deeply ingrained habit.

It's likely that the majority of people who ever knew Chester have some story of his giving which few others know about, and after Chester's death it was fun to hear some of those stories surface even decades after they happened. During the last days of Chester's life, his wife mentioned to me that years ago Chester had a young man working with him on one of his oil rigs. Chester found out about the young man's desire to go to college. Rather than just wishing him luck and getting back to work, Chester told the boy, "I'll put you through school."

Then he did.

Chester didn't flaunt his generosity, so I won't tell more stories of it here, but generosity was a habit for him, something that was ingrained in him deeply enough that it wasn't at all difficult for him to give for the good of others.

Some of the moments with Chester that I'll always cherish the most were in the last years of his life, when even though his health was declining, it gave me more chances than I'd had ever had before to just sit with him

Day 14: Thursday

and hear stories of his life. One story from his childhood helped me to understand where his generosity came from:

He said that as a boy he was walking to town with his father one day. His father always kept a dollar bill folded up in his shirt pocket. As they were walking, a man came up to them saying that he was hungry, needed help and didn't have any money to buy food, so Chester's father took the dollar bill from his pocket and gave it to the man.

As they kept walking, Chester said that he asked his father why he did that since it was the only dollar they had with them, and his father told him simply that the man asked for help, and he could help, so he gave the dollar.

Later in the day, as they made their walk back home, they walked past a saloon and saw the man to whom they'd given the dollar inside the saloon drinking. Chester said that he got angry and pointed the man out to his dad. His father's response was, "That's okay, son. If you give a dollar to a hundred people, ninety-nine of them might go do something like that. But think of the difference you'd make to the one who really needs it."

I know some who have decided to give to agencies rather than giving money to individuals, but regardless of how each of us decides to approach this, it's clear that generosity should be one of our marks as Jesus' followers. In his kingdom, we have no reason to fear being taken advantage of, so we are free to pursue being generous. We often try to make ourselves into generous people, but then we just revert back to being as we always were. With Chester, for whom–by the time I knew him–it was more natural to be generous than to be stingy, he never had to grit his teeth and make himself give to others while he really wanted to keep things for himself. No, his generosity began with a story like this that was deeply ingrained in him and shaped his habits throughout his life. By the time I came along, giving to others was so deeply-seated in him that it was a natural part of his character.

A Prayer for the Day:
Heavenly Father, in you we live and move and have our being: We humbly pray you so to guide and govern us by your Holy Spirit, that in all the cares and occupations of our life we may not forget you, but may remember that we are ever walking in your sight; through Jesus Christ our Lord. Amen.

A Prayer for the Week:
Almighty God, you know that we have no power in ourselves to help ourselves: Keep us both outwardly in our bodies and inwardly in our souls, that we may be defended from all adversities which may happen to the body, and from all evil thoughts which may assault and hurt the soul; through Jesus Christ our Lord, who lives and reigns with you and the Holy Spirit, one God, for ever and ever. Amen.

Day 15: Friday

Why We Don't Give in a Hurry

The church I belong to once hosted a very helpful visit from Dr. Richard Swenson. Swenson is a physician who is best known for helping people become aware of our need for what he calls *margin*. In his excellent book, *Margin: Restoring Emotional, Physical, Financial, and Time Reserves to Overloaded Lives*, Swenson defines margin as "the space between our load and our limits," suggesting that many of us are carrying loads that are beyond our limits in the four areas in his title, and his prescription is that we function best when we leave margin between the loads we carry and the limits that we naturally face as human beings.

Our discussion this week about Jesus' statement, "When you give…" brought to mind a story that Dr. Swenson told us during his visit. He said that a group of researchers did a study on seminary students. These seminarians were told that they were given the assignment of giving a talk in a nearby room, and some of them received the task of explaining Jesus' parable of the Good Samaritan (see Luke 10:25-37). There were two variables in the study: the sense of hurry that was created for the students, and what they were given to think about. Some were told that they were already running late and had actually been expected a few minutes ago. Others were told their audience was ready for them and that they should go right over into the other room. A third group was told that it would be a few minutes before their audience would be ready, but they might as well head over to the other room.

On the students' way from one room to another on their campus to give their talks, they each individually encountered a person lying in a doorway, doubled over, with eyes closed and coughing. The researchers' hypothesis was that the two variables would be very influential in whether or not students would stop to help. They thought that the student's sense of hurry and their mindset would matter more than personality differences or religious commitment or other such factors. They were exactly right. Of the seminary students who had some margin, who had been told they had a few minutes to spare, 63% stopped to help. Of those who were not early, but on time, 45% stopped to help. Of those running late, only 10% stopped to give any help to the obviously struggling person in the door. The study noted that some of the students even stepped over the apparently injured person. And half of these students were on their way to give a talk *on the Good Samaritan!*[17]

The lesson we must learn from this is, regardless of our level of Christian devotion, we are much less likely to give of ourselves to others–whether it be through giving our time, resources, or other ways–when we are in a hurry. Hurry is an interior condition brought on when we feel threatened, but even though Jesus' threats were so real throughout his life–particularly on his way to Jerusalem and the cross–we never get the sense that he

Day 15: Friday

was in a hurry. Rather, he knew that despite the cross that awaited him, he was ultimately safe in God's kingdom.

So am I, and so are you. And that is why we can live and give at a kingdom pace. In tomorrow's final reflection on "When you give…," we'll take a closer look at how the reality of God's kingdom affects our giving.

A Prayer for the Day:
Almighty God, whose most dear Son went not up to joy but first he suffered pain, and entered not into glory before he was crucified: Mercifully grant that we, walking in the way of the cross, may find it none other than the way of life and peace; through Jesus Christ our Lord. Amen.

A Prayer for the Week:
Almighty God, you know that we have no power in ourselves to help ourselves: Keep us both outwardly in our bodies and inwardly in our souls, that we may be defended from all adversities which may happen to the body, and from all evil thoughts which may assault and hurt the soul; through Jesus Christ our Lord, who lives and reigns with you and the Holy Spirit, one God, for ever and ever. Amen.

Day 16: Saturday

Big Spending and Over-Saving vs. Contentment and Generosity

Apparently some of us are wired to be big spenders, while others of us are over-savers. Regardless of which side of that spectrum you may lean toward, we can all become a third type of person: someone who lives in contentment and generosity.

Yet contentment and generosity don't become ours by accident. In a world like the one in which you and I live, they have to be cultivated. Studies say that we receive an average of 600 advertising messages every day, and it's safe to say that every one of those is pulling us toward being a big spender (*You have to buy your wife this big diamond or she may not kiss you any more*), or an over-saver (*You need to invest now in gold, because the entire economy could collapse around us–then at least if it did…well, you would own some gold*). I have yet to see any advertisement whose point is, "Be content with what you have so that you can be more generous to others."

So if contentment and generosity are qualities we desire for ourselves, we need to pursue them resolutely. As Jesus indicated several verses after he said "When

Day 16: Saturday

you give…," the way that we pursue these qualities is by seeking God's kingdom.

But what in the world does it mean to seek God's kingdom, how are we supposed to do it, and how does it help us become content and generous?

Perhaps the simplest summary of the meaning of God's kingdom is that it is what God is doing in our world. If God is king in any meaningful sense, surely he has say over some things and is active in some way. So when we seek God's kingdom, we seek to understand what God is doing–in our own lives, around the world, and in all of creation throughout history.

To seek the kingdom, then, we pay attention to the same three areas that we constantly develop as Jesus' followers: our minds, our habits, and our relationships.

Then, once we begin taking next steps in each of those areas (which usually make themselves obvious to us when we start looking for them), over time we will notice something: characteristics like contentment and generosity are no longer things that we have to grit our teeth and try to force. Rather, they begin to come naturally. We might even be surprised at how easy they become, all because we've begun to learn to live in God's kingdom.

There is nothing wrong with spending on things we need–or even on some of the things we want, and it is wise for us to save some money for future expenses. Yet in God's kingdom, we become convinced of the truth of those opening words of Psalm 23: the Lord God is our shepherd, and therefore we will not lack anything. We no longer need to over-spend on clothes to get people to think of us in the right way. We no longer need to over-save, as if our futures were in our own hands rather than in God's. No, when we train ourselves to notice how abundantly generous God is, each day, toward us, then our fears begin to be laid aside and our big spending and over-saving will naturally become transformed into contentment and generosity.

A Prayer for the Day:

Almighty God, who after the creation of the world rested from all your works and sanctified a day of rest for all your creatures: Grant that we, putting away all earthly anxieties, may be duly prepared for the service of your sanctuary, and that our rest here upon earth may be a preparation for the eternal rest promised to your people in heaven; through Jesus Christ our Lord. Amen.

A Prayer for the Week:

Almighty God, you know that we have no power in ourselves to help ourselves: Keep us both outwardly in our bodies and inwardly in our souls, that we may be defended from all adversities which may happen to the body, and from all evil thoughts which may assault and hurt the soul; through Jesus Christ our Lord, who lives and reigns with you and the Holy Spirit, one God, for ever and ever. Amen.

Day 17: Monday

Don't Pray to be Seen by Others

If you have ever been part of any Christian group that ended its times together by someone saying a prayer, you've probably experienced something like this:

Person in charge: *Okay. Anyone want to say the prayer?*

[Silence]

Person in charge: *C'mon. It's no big deal. Somebody?*

[Silence that's more awkward, with increased fidgeting]

Someone in the group, who also said the prayer the previous three weeks: *[Sigh] I'll do it…*

I grew up participating in this routine in Sunday School classes, youth group meetings, etc., and somewhere along the line the impression was given to me that it was a mark of maturity in our lives as Christians to be the one willing to heave the sigh, say "I'll do it," and then say the prayer so that the awkwardness could be over and everyone could leave. If that was true, then it was a mark of super-maturity whenever someone would skip the awkwardness, fidgeting, and sighing to volunteer themselves immediately upon the request. (Or perhaps, if not maturity, it was a mark that they were in a hurry to get to the dessert, or the football game, or whatever was happening next.)

Since I had a sincere desire to live as God wanted, and being the one willing to say the prayer was part of my picture of a mature Christian, somewhere along the line I decided I would be one of those willing to pray aloud whenever the awkward silence reached a certain level without anyone else volunteering to do it. That willingness opened the door to a whole other set of popular prayer games. As I got further into my teenage years, I began to make friends with others who were also willing to be the ones to say the prayers. Again, out of our young sincere desire to please God, we would sometimes arrange ourselves in groups to do this kind of praying together, and I discovered something interesting: in that kind of setting, the expectation changed from someone in the group being willing to say the prayer to everyone in the group being required to say a prayer. If we didn't pray anything aloud, it would obviously mean we didn't love Jesus very much.

Once I figured that out, and was praying aloud every time it was my turn so that no one would have cause to doubt my love of God, another level opened up to me. If I said things in my prayer that others in my "we're-willing-to-pray-aloud" group really liked, they would respond–right there as I was praying! Everyone seemed to have their own way of doing it. For some, it was a "Yes, Jesus," or "Yes, Lord." Others might give a more conservative "Amen." The most common response seemed to be an "Mmmmm," which I learned to translate as, "I really like what he just said."

I no longer accept anyone's willingness to pray aloud as an indicator of their love for God. Nor do I have any

Day 17: Monday

problem with people who have their own verbal way of agreeing with a prayer that someone else has said. The problem that I have in looking back on those experiences is with *me*. Yes, I meant the things I said in the prayers, but I was paying at least as much attention to the reactions of the people hearing me–even calculating my words in order to try to get a reaction from them–as I was paying attention to God.

In those days, I didn't know these words of Jesus as well as I do now:

And when you pray, do not be like the hypocrites, for they love to pray standing in the synagogues and on the street corners to be seen by others. Truly I tell you, they have received their reward in full. But when you pray, go into your room, close the door and pray to your Father, who is unseen. Then your Father, who sees what is done in secret, will reward you. And when you pray, do not keep on babbling like pagans, for they think they will be heard because of their many words. Do not be like them, for your Father knows what you need before you ask him. (Matthew 6:5-8, NIV)

These days, apparently, I usually pray with more reserved people than I did back then because–even though I still do pray aloud in different contexts fairly regularly–those kinds of reactions don't happen as often as they used to. But I'm fine with that. Thankfully, I've come to see the point of our praying as enabling us to live prayerful lives rather than trying to see who can get the most "Mmmm"s and "Yes Lord"s in the prayer meeting. Throughout the rest of this week, we'll look at three ways of praying that can be helpful when we attempt to follow up on Jesus' "when you pray…"

instructions: praying with other people's words, praying without words, and praying with our own words.[18]

A Prayer for the Day:
O God, the King eternal, whose light divides the day from the night and turns the shadow of death into the morning: Drive far from us all wrong desires, incline our hearts to keep your law, and guide our feet into the way of peace; that, having done your will with cheerfulness while it was day, we may, when night comes, rejoice to give you thanks; through Jesus Christ our Lord. Amen.

A Prayer for the Week:
Gracious Father, whose blessed Son Jesus Christ came down from heaven to be the true bread which gives life to the world: Evermore give us this bread, that he may live in us, and we in him; who lives and reigns with you and the Holy Spirit, one God, now and for ever. Amen.

Day 18: Tuesday

The Prayer Jesus Taught Us

Certainly, as followers of Christ, no other prayer is as central to us as the one that Jesus taught us. I know of no sense in which we can call ourselves followers of Jesus without taking very seriously the words he gave us when he said, "When you pray, pray like this, 'Our Father, who art in heaven…'"

One way that I have found particularly helpful to be guided by Jesus' prayer is to allow it to focus my prayers for others and for myself. For example, let's say I am praying for my children. I can pray for them by saying,

Our Father in heaven, and be mindful and thankful that whether I'm with them or away from them, that God is present with and caring for them just as he is present with and caring for me.

I pray, *hallowed be thy name*, and I'm praying that God's name would be treasured and honored in their lives and in mine.

And I continue on through the prayer, being mindful of praying it for the other person. Then I can pray, *Thy kingdom come, thy will be done on earth, in my children and in our family, just as it is in heaven*, praying that their lives in this world, today and always would be an extension of God's life among us.

And I pray, *Give us this day our daily bread*, praying that my little boy and my little girl would have all of the things they need today to live their lives fully in God: physically, emotionally, spiritually, relationally, in every way.

Forgive us our trespasses as we forgive those who trespass against us...My children are now at the age that, regardless of what time of day you might be reading this, they've likely already built a list of things for which they need forgiveness. As I pray this for them, I am praying particularly that they would always know our home to be a place of forgiveness and mercy. They're going to mess up, and by praying this I'm in part praying that when that time comes, I'll be a forgiving father to them just as my Father has forgiven me.

Lead us not into temptation, but deliver us from evil. What better thing to pray for your children, or for whomever, than that they would be led along, not in the ways of the world around them, but in God's ways, and that they would be completely and fully delivered from all the kinds of evil that will ever be a threat to them every day of their lives?

For thine is the kingdom, the power, and the glory forever. These kids are my children, yet they are God's children. Just as my name is on the line in their lives, because we've entrusted them to God, his name is on the line with them too, and so I pray that their lives will, today and always, give him glory.

It's interesting that we know even as early as 60 A.D., within a generation of Jesus' own life, even before much of the New Testament had been written, Christians were being instructed to pray these words of Jesus three times a day. Certainly we can benefit from doing the same, and perhaps you'd like to take up that practice for the remainder of Lent, realizing when you pray these words, you're joining together with millions of other Christians around the world praying them today, and throughout history, all around the world.[19]

A Prayer for the Day:
O God, the author of peace and lover of concord, to know you is eternal life and to serve you is perfect freedom: Defend us, your humble servants, in all assaults of our enemies; that we, surely trusting in your defense, may not fear the power of any adversaries; through the might of Jesus Christ our Lord. Amen.

A Prayer for the Week:
Gracious Father, whose blessed Son Jesus Christ came down from heaven to be the true bread which gives life to the world: Evermore give us this bread, that he may live in us, and we in him; who lives and reigns with you and the Holy Spirit, one God, now and for ever. Amen.

Day 19: Wednesday

The Prayer David Left Us

Many of the stories of Jesus' life that you and I may be able to bring to mind are associated with Lent. We are in the midst of considering part of his famous Sermon on the Mount, which, among many other well-known things he said, includes the passages that are giving shape to three weeks of these reflections (When you give…When you pray…When you fast…). If you think of which biblical stories come to mind when you think of Lent, you might remember some of these: Jesus' temptation in the wilderness, his entrance into Jerusalem riding on a donkey while the crowds cheered, a woman anointing him with expensive perfume, Judas' betrayal, the washing of the disciples' feet, the Last Supper, and certainly Jesus' arrest, trial, crucifixion, and burial.

These are the stories that shape Lent for us each year. But this week, as we consider prayer–particularly in continuing to look at praying with other people's words–what are the prayers that shape Lent for us? Is there any prayer from the Bible that comes to mind when you think of Lent?

For me, it is Psalm 51, the prayer of repentance, which tradition has ascribed to David after being confronted by the prophet Nathan about his sin with Bathsheba. (Take a

Day 19: Wednesday

few minutes to read it now, slowly, if you can.) It is the psalm we are given to begin Lent each year on Ash Wednesday. It is given to us every year for good reason, as it expresses the desire that has drawn so many Christians into Lenten practices throughout the centuries.

This prayer is:

- a totally exposed, gut-wrenched plea to God for mercy on our transgressions while also expressing a profound trust in his unfailing love and great compassion;

- an acknowledgement of our own utter helplessness when it comes to ridding ourselves of sin and washing away its stains;

- a view of ourselves as standing before God, our loving and just judge, and each entering our plea of "guilty–though you have always known that and have loved me anyway";

- an expression of hope in God as the only one who can guide us through the mess that we have created for ourselves;

- a recognition that, while it's possible to do all of the helpful outward things in ways that look good, in the end the only thing that truly opens the door to restoration for us is having hearts that are continually repentant in ways that only God can see;

- an awareness of our public privilege and responsibility, once we have been restored, to also help point others toward the same reconciliation that God has so generously offered us (time after time, after time, after time…).

This prayer is given to us so that it can shape our own praying. Two of the most important benefits of praying with other people's words are:
1. Those aren't the kinds of things I usually come up with to pray about on my own, though when I pray them, they resonate with me as being things that match my soul-level desires.
2. I am not the first person to pray these words. From the time of David on, God's people have found them fitting to pray as a way of acknowledging our sin and seeking God's mercy. Faithful Jews prayed them while in exile and waiting for the Messiah. Mary and Joseph prayed them. So did Peter, James, John, Paul, and all of the rest of the early Christians. So did countless others through the centuries–from St. Augustine to St. Francis to Martin Luther to Martin Luther King Jr., from John of the Cross to John Wesley…to you and me as we are privileged to pray them together today.

A Prayer for the Day:
Lord God, almighty and everlasting Father, you have brought us in safety to this new day: Preserve us with your mighty power, that we may not fall into sin, nor be overcome by adversity; and in all we do, direct us to the fulfilling of your purpose; through Jesus Christ our Lord. Amen.

A Prayer for the Week:
Gracious Father, whose blessed Son Jesus Christ came down from heaven to be the true bread which gives life to the world: Evermore give us this bread, that he may live in us, and we in him; who lives and reigns with you and the Holy Spirit, one God, now and for ever. Amen.

Day 20: Thursday

The Prayer Someone Gave Manasseh

Perhaps at some point you have noticed something that can seem very confusing: some groups of Christians have Bibles that include more books than other groups of Christians. Growing up as a Protestant, somewhere along the line I picked up on the implicit message that groups who had the "extra books" really must not care very much about the accurately preserving the Bible (or–for that matter–must not care very much about God).

Boy, was I wrong. My first clue that the extra books (the best term for them is "Deuterocanonical books," or in the past they were referred to as the "Apocrypha," but I'll stick with "extra" since it's easier to type) have some good things to say was when I bought a study Bible edited by a group of my favorite Christian scholars, and they decided to include the extra books.[20] In part of their explanation of why they did so while knowing it would be a change for most of their readers, they explained that while these books aren't given the same weight as other parts of the Bible, they are worth reading and can be helpful to us just as good sermons and devotional writings. Even Martin Luther himself said, "Apocrypha–

that is, books which are not regarded as equal to the holy scriptures, and yet are profitable and good to read."

(I've probably made this explanation longer than necessary for today's reflection, but hopefully–if you come from a background similar to mine–it will at least convince you there's no need to call an exorcist the next time you see one of the extra-books-Bibles.)

My second step toward valuing these books came when I started having a regular method for praying with other people's words by using prayer books. I've most often used *The Book of Common Prayer*, and about once every couple of weeks, I come around to this prayer from one of the extra books, "Prayer of Manasseh," which is a great prayer and provides a good direction for my prayers during Lent:

O Lord and Ruler of the hosts of heaven,
God of Abraham, Isaac, and Jacob,
and of all their righteous offspring:
You made the heavens and the earth,
with all their vast array.

All things quake with fear at your presence;
they tremble because of your power.
But your merciful promise is beyond all measure;
it surpasses all that our minds can fathom.
O Lord, you are full of compassion,
long-suffering, and abounding in mercy.
You hold back your hand;
you do not punish as we deserve.
In your great goodness, Lord,
you have promised forgiveness to sinners,
that they may repent of their sin and be saved.
And now, O Lord, I bend the knee of my heart,
and make my appeal, sure of your gracious goodness.

Day 20: Thursday

I have sinned, O Lord, I have sinned,
and I know my wickedness only too well.
Therefore I make this prayer to you:
Forgive me, Lord, forgive me.
Do not let me perish in my sin,
nor condemn me to the depths of the earth.
For you, O Lord, are the God of those who repent,
and in me you will show forth your goodness.
Unworthy as I am, you will save me,
in accordance with your great mercy,
and I will praise you without ceasing
all the days of my life.
For all the powers of heaven sing your praises,
and yours is the glory to ages of ages. Amen.
(Prayer of Manasseh 1-2, 4, 6-7, 11-15)[21]

That's a good prayer, regardless of which kind of Bible you have. It's ascribed to Manasseh, who–though he almost certainly didn't actually write it, which is part of the reason why it's one of the extra books rather than the regular books–was the longest reigning monarch of Judah, and a *really, really* bad one. Yet before the end of his life, he turned back to God with a prayer of repentance, so we follow the good part of his example by praying rich words like those of this prayer. (See 2 Chronicles 33:1-20 for Manasseh's story.)

A Prayer for the Day:

Heavenly Father, in you we live and move and have our being: We humbly pray you so to guide and govern us by your Holy Spirit, that in all the cares and occupations of our life we may not forget you, but may remember that we are ever walking in your sight; through Jesus Christ our Lord. Amen.

A Prayer for the Week:

Gracious Father, whose blessed Son Jesus Christ came down from heaven to be the true bread which gives life to the world: Evermore give us this bread, that he may live in us, and we in him; who lives and reigns with you and the Holy Spirit, one God, now and for ever. Amen.

Day 21: Friday

A Greatly Needed (and Little Experienced) Challenge

One of my mentors, Ruth Haley Barton, has written, "silence is the most challenging, the most needed and the least experienced spiritual discipline among evangelical Christians today."[22] That's quite a big statement, but I think she's right. If being quiet with God by praying without words is the most challenging, the most needed, and the least experienced spiritual discipline for us today, it's going to be stretching for all of us, regardless of our personality preferences.

Praying without words is a practice that is contrary to our feelings, and it's going to stretch any of us who practice it, so why would we bother with it?

Maybe we can understand the need for practicing prayer without words in our relationship with God if we think of times without words with our loved ones. Something about our relationships helps us to understand that it can be a sign of maturity to be able to enjoy being together while not saying anything.

My father was my hero, and he was extremely quiet. When I graduated from high school, I had the idea that it would be fun for the two of us to make the six-hour drive to the Dallas-Fort Worth Metroplex to see a Texas Rangers baseball game together. Their new ballpark had just opened, and he'd never been to a major league game, so we went. He and I drove there in his pickup truck the day of the game, watched it, stayed the night in a hotel, drove back the next day, and I don't think we said more than 150 words on the whole trip. And for the rest of his life we still mentioned how much we enjoyed that trip!

You are likely not as quiet as my father and I, but I think you can understand something of this aspect of a relationship between people. There comes a point in getting to know someone when you can enjoy just being together rather than having to get acquainted through small talk and other conversation. Sure, words are still fine and are often used, but there is also a trust and comfort that is uniquely expressed without them.

Brennan Manning says, "Simply showing up is a kind of loving. The readiness to conscientiously waste time with a friend is a silent affirmation of their importance in our lives."[23] That is a great description of what prayer without words is: conscientiously wasting time with a friend to affirm their importance in our lives.

I had been a Christian for quite a while before I ever realized the truth of this in my relationship with God. It occurred to me, "If I cannot enjoy just being with God, without having to fill the time with words or other things, what does that say about how close we are? How can I even really describe it as a relationship, much less an 'intimate personal relationship' like we often say, if I will so easily come up with any tool or excuse available to avoid just being with God?"

Day 21: Friday

Dallas Willard describes this bluntly. He says, "Silence is frightening because it strips us as nothing else does, throwing us upon the stark realities of our life. It reminds us of death, which will cut us off from this world and leave only us and God. And in that quiet, what if there turns out to be very little to 'just us and God'? Think of what it says about the emptiness of our inner lives if we must always turn on the tape player or radio to make sure something is happening around us."[24]

Praying without any words is such an important part of the spiritual life because our time in prayer without words is the time when that "something between just me and God" is given a chance to grow and develop. It is the time when what we so often call a relationship with God can come to consist of the two of us actually enjoying being together.[25]

A Prayer for the Day:
Almighty God, whose most dear Son went not up to joy but first he suffered pain, and entered not into glory before he was crucified: Mercifully grant that we, walking in the way of the cross, may find it none other than the way of life and peace; through Jesus Christ our Lord. Amen.

A Prayer for the Week:
Gracious Father, whose blessed Son Jesus Christ came down from heaven to be the true bread which gives life to the world: Evermore give us this bread, that he may live in us, and we in him; who lives and reigns with you and the Holy Spirit, one God, now and for ever. Amen.

Day 22: Saturday

I Hope I Never Forget This Conversation With My Son

I recently bought a bigger pickup truck, solely for the purpose of being able to take my kids around with me when I'm doing work on our ranch. I love it when I get to take them. Sure, my productivity takes a dramatic nosedive, but I can still get some things done, and I love having my favorite people (my family) with me at my favorite place (our ranch).

I had my three-year-old son with me on one of these days, and on our way out of town driving toward the ranch we had to stop at a tire shop and get a flat tire fixed. After it was finished, and as I was buckling my little boy back into his car seat, we had a short conversation that I hope I never forget:

Me: I sure love having you with me, Bud.

Him: I love having you with me, too, Daddy. I wouldn't want to go anywhere without ya.

…[He thought for a minute as I continued buckling him in]…

Him: If you were going somewhere by yourself, I'd want to catch up.

A comment like *that* will make any daddy's day. In fact, that conversation took place more than a year ago, so I guess I can say that it didn't just make my day, but made my year.

Out of the three ways of praying that we have explored this week, and which are described further in *Live Prayerfully*, I grew up most accustomed to this third way, praying with my own words. Although it was the most familiar to me when I was younger (and there's a good chance that's also the case for many of you reading this), in recent years I've focused more on the other two ways of praying.

Praying with other people's words through practices like Fixed-Hour Prayer has brought a shape, rhythm and depth to my prayer practices for which I had longed for years.

Praying without words seems to be one of the most needed practices in my own spiritual life, and probably is for many of us. It's in doing so that what we so often call "a personal relationship with God," for me, becomes something that can actually be described as a relationship.

But these comments from my little boy, and the immense joy that they brought to me, knowing that they came from a very sincere place in his tender little heart, have reminded me of the power of talking to God in very personal words. For a lot of people, this is a very natural and easy way to pray, but it's not always for me, at least not at this point in my life.

I don't know if my words to God can have anywhere close to the same effect on him that my son's can have on me, but I would guess that it's similar. It certainly isn't by accident that the writers of scripture, and particularly

Jesus, so often choose to describe our relationship to God as one between a loving father and his children. So, if things between God and me are similar to things between my son and me, I need to tell him how much I like being with him.

It doesn't require many words, but I've got to use some.[26]

A Prayer for the Day:
Almighty God, who after the creation of the world rested from all your works and sanctified a day of rest for all your creatures: Grant that we, putting away all earthly anxieties, may be duly prepared for the service of your sanctuary, and that our rest here upon earth may be a preparation for the eternal rest promised to your people in heaven; through Jesus Christ our Lord. Amen.

A Prayer for the Week:
Gracious Father, whose blessed Son Jesus Christ came down from heaven to be the true bread which gives life to the world: Evermore give us this bread, that he may live in us, and we in him; who lives and reigns with you and the Holy Spirit, one God, now and for ever. Amen.

Day 23: Monday

Don't Fast to be Seen by Others

Two weeks ago, we looked at implications of Jesus' instructions when he said, "When you give…," and I began that week by telling a somewhat embarrassing story about a time when I've done exactly the opposite of what Jesus taught. Then, last week, we looked at implications of Jesus' instructions when he said, "When you pray…," and I began with a somewhat embarrassing story about a time when I've done exactly the opposite of what Jesus taught. This week, we look at implications of Jesus' instructions when he said, "When you fast…," and rather than an embarrassing story, I can only give more of a confession: I haven't practiced this one enough to have many stories–embarrassing or otherwise.

It isn't that I've never fasted. It seems like each year, usually during Lent, I have some different way of experimenting with it. So, I have enough experience with fasting to try to write six helpful reflections for this week. Yet I still feel a hesitation about writing anything about it, and perhaps that comes less from a lack of experience than it does from the knowledge that any efforts I've ever made in this practice have all been–at best–

stumbling, bumbling efforts to which I can imagine God lovingly saying, "Well, thanks for trying."

One of my first and most memorable experiences with fasting was in graduate school. It was an introductory Spiritual Formation course in which we were studying and practicing different classic spiritual disciplines. When we received the syllabus, I noticed that the instructor had planned a week on fasting, which included the assignment of a three-day fast. I wasn't looking forward to it, but I had it on my radar, which was apparently better than a good number of my classmates. When we got to that week in the course, several of my peers who hadn't read the syllabus very closely did their best to virtually stage a revolt against the professor. *How in the world could he expect us to do that?* It became apparent that many of us enjoyed learning about and practicing spiritual disciplines until it came to one which was very effective at making us uncomfortable.

The professor gently guided us back to the fact that we all should have paid closer attention to the syllabus, and he also pointed us to Jesus' statement we're considering this week, not *"if* you fast," but *"when* you fast." Then, we all felt better when he assured us that the course requirement was that we *attempt* the three-day fast, not necessarily that we *complete* it. Many of my classmates gave up within the first day. I was much more mature than them and made it about 25 hours before throwing in the towel.

We have our subtle ways of giving to be seen by others, or praying to be seen by others, but our religious culture today is so far removed from that of Jesus, that fasting to be seen by others would be pretty obnoxious to

Day 23: Monday

most of us rather than being tempting. So perhaps Jesus' instructions about not fasting in order to be seen by others are way too easy for us today. Our work-around for it is simple: if we never fast, we're never fasting to be seen by others.

But still, Jesus' statement implies that his followers will fast, and in another place (Matthew 9:14-15), Jesus even says explicitly that–after he is taken from them–his followers *will* fast. Many of Jesus' friends throughout the centuries have found this practice to be so deeply *good* that the church continues to hang on to its importance, even though many of us today have almost completely laid it aside.

So, for this week's reflections on our journey of denying ourselves and following Jesus toward the cross, let's all put on our steel-toe boots, realize that this is a practice *designed* to make us uncomfortable, and know that our loving, gracious Lord and millions of his friends have all walked this way before us.

Tomorrow we'll consider why it makes sense for fasting to have a place in our lives with God. Wednesday and Thursday, we'll look at the traditional practice of fasting from food, including its place in the Bible and in Christian history, with the early Methodists as a case study. We'll conclude the week by looking at other types of fasting, where we abstain from things other than food.

A Prayer for the Day:

O God, the King eternal, whose light divides the day from the night and turns the shadow of death into the morning: Drive far from us all wrong desires, incline our hearts to keep your law, and guide our feet into the way of peace; that, having done your will with cheerfulness while it was day, we may, when night comes, rejoice to give you thanks; through Jesus Christ our Lord. Amen.

A Prayer for the Week:

Almighty God, you alone can bring into order the unruly wills and affections of sinners: Grant your people grace to love what you command and desire what you promise; that, among the swift and varied changes of the world, our hearts may surely there be fixed where true joys are to be found; through Jesus Christ our Lord, who lives and reigns with you and the Holy Spirit, one God, now and for ever. Amen.

Day 24: Tuesday

Why Your Spiritual Practices Might Be Wearing You Out

From the time I was a child, I have been extremely privileged to be around devout Christians who have modeled life with God for me very well. At every stage of my life, I have had people who encouraged me and invited me deeper into the kind of life available to all of us in God's kingdom.

When I was old enough to begin taking some responsibility for the quality of my own life with God, I began trying to do the things that we are taught to do as Christians–activities like prayer, reading my Bible, and worship. Though it didn't take much experience with those practices to know that they could be beneficial, for years–probably even decades–I found that my motivation to do them was very inconsistent. It would wax and wane, as I would be dedicated for a while, then get tired and hardly practice anything. Then the cycle would repeat itself.

I didn't understand why that happened. I thought, "Perhaps I just wasn't as committed to God as I hoped. I really need to be serious next time. (But maybe not just yet)." Then I heard one of my heroes, Dallas Willard, say something which made it click for me. It took the pressure off, and has helped me tremendously in arranging my life around my desire for God in the years since. Before telling you what Dallas' statement was, I need to set up its context.

Most of the things you and I have usually been taught are important practices in the lives of people who are seeking the kingdom of God are "doing" things. Practices like those I mentioned above–prayer, Bible study, and worship, as well as others such as service and fellowship–are all things we *do*, or we could say more accurately, they are practices that require our engagement. For those decades of my life before I heard Dallas' statement, somewhere between ninety and one hundred percent of my spiritual practices were in this category. I read my Bible, prayed, worshipped, served others, met with groups, and generally gave myself a very full plate of Christian activity. Though these things were good, I did them to the point where I had no energy left for them. I came to resent (at times) meeting with groups rather than doing the other things I thought I really wanted to be doing. My interest in and energy for prayer, reading the scriptures, and worship were like a roller coaster.

Now, back to Dallas' statement: He said that to have only disciplines of engagement without also having disciplines of abstinence is a recipe for burnout.[27]

Though it may not appear to be so on first glance, it's a brilliant observation. I had a cycle of wearing myself out with spiritual practices, because they were all of the "doing things" type (disciplines of engagement). I had virtually nothing in my life with God that was a practice of "not doing" (disciplines of abstinence).

Day 24: Tuesday

So what are the disciplines of abstinence, the things that we intentionally do not do, for the sake of opening ourselves to God's work? Every person's list may be different, but things like sleep, Sabbath, and simple living are important, refreshing practices for most of us. The church has also held on to three other practices through the centuries that fall into this category, because they are so consistently effective at helping us become more open to God: solitude, silence, and fasting.

Since Jesus' statement, "When you fast...," is our focus for this week, and since in yesterday's post I talked about how much it makes us uncomfortable, perhaps it can help us let our defenses down before looking at the practice the rest of the week to look at it in this context. As one of the central practices of abstinence for us, part of its role is to refresh us and help us to rest. It's a practice which, though uncomfortable, is an invitation rather than a demand.

As I mentioned yesterday, my experiences with fasting are still fairly limited, but since hearing Dallas' statement and intentionally letting practices of "not doing" (disciplines of abstinence) have more of a place in my life, my desire for life with God and energy for pursuing it stay much more consistent. We need to engage, and we need to abstain–both for the purpose of remaining open to God's work of grace.

Tomorrow we will take a surprising look at fasting in the Bible, and then on Thursday and Friday, at fasting in the Methodist tradition. We will look at them in the light that this statement from Dallas Willard shed on why many of us get worn out by our practices and how fasting and other "not doing" practices help us to avoid getting there.

Follow

A Prayer for the Day:
O God, the author of peace and lover of concord, to know you is eternal life and to serve you is perfect freedom: Defend us, your humble servants, in all assaults of our enemies; that we, surely trusting in your defense, may not fear the power of any adversaries; through the might of Jesus Christ our Lord. Amen.

A Prayer for the Week:
Almighty God, you alone can bring into order the unruly wills and affections of sinners: Grant your people grace to love what you command and desire what you promise; that, among the swift and varied changes of the world, our hearts may surely there be fixed where true joys are to be found; through Jesus Christ our Lord, who lives and reigns with you and the Holy Spirit, one God, now and for ever. Amen.

Day 25: Wednesday

Fasting in the Bible: Not a Way to Twist God's Arm

One pendulum that has swung in Christian teaching over our lifetimes is the quantity of teaching and writing on the topic of fasting. In the first helpful material I ever read on fasting, Richard Foster's chapter on this practice in *Celebration of Discipline*, he noted, "in my research I could not find a single book published on the subject of Christian fasting from 1861 to 1954, a period of nearly 100 years."[28] Today, in contrast, I just did a quick search online which turned up 157 current Christian books with fasting as their subject matter.

In scanning through the list, I only see three that I have read, and honestly–I have no desire to ever read a good portion of them. While I'll give the authors the benefit of the doubt and assume they say some good things, just judging by the titles, there are many which I think fail to reflect what fasting was in the Bible. To illustrate, just from the titles of books on this list, these are things which we are led to believe can/should come if we practice fasting:

- power
- miracles

- breakthroughs of different kinds (spiritual, emotional, physical, and–of course–even financial)
- health, energy and longer life
- better preaching
- revival
- and the one that takes the prize, from one of the book descriptions: "achieving your dreams at 'break neck' speed"

It seems like we have turned this biblical practice into a way of twisting God's arm into giving us something that, by our fasting, we are showing him that we *really, really* want. It's kind of like our spiritualized adult version of a toddler's attempts at manipulating their parents by throwing a temper tantrum. "God, I *really* want this, and I'm going to prove it to you by going without food for a while."

Author and New Testament scholar Scot McKnight has written a fantastic book (simply titled *Fasting*) which provides a much-needed corrective, focusing on what fasting was in the Bible. From the book's introduction to conclusion, he directly addresses this misconception of fasting and continually reiterates that in the scriptures, fasting is our appropriate response to God, and/or to some part of life, *not* "a manipulative tool that guarantees results."[29]

So instead of fasting *for* something, biblically, we are given the model of fasting as a response. There are times in life when filling our mouths is out of line and fasting is the natural, appropriate way to express our reaction in a whole-person kind of way by including our bodies in the response. For example, perhaps we lose a loved one and we fast as a way of grieving (2 Samuel 1:1-12). Or, at

Day 25: Wednesday

times we certainly have a profound need to plead before God on behalf of others (Deuteronomy 9:15-21). We may become more deeply aware of those suffering in poverty or injustice (Isaiah 58:3-12). Certainly there will be times when we are overcome by our need for repentance (1 Samuel 7:3-6). Plus, Lent is–in part–a continuation of the ancient Jewish practice of regularly observing days when a particular response to God is appropriate (Leviticus 16:29-30).

If our understanding of what fasting is has drifted this far from what it was in the Bible, it shouldn't be any surprise to us that we have more trouble with Jesus saying "when you fast…" than we do with him saying "when you give…" or "when you pray…." Part of our problem, which McKnight addresses so well in his book and as I've hinted at in previous days' readings, is that we have come to view our bodies as having little or no roles in our "spiritual" lives. Many of us even think of our bodies as being opposed to living the kind of lives that God wants. It's true that our bodies need to be trained, like every other part of us, but they are given to us as allies, or our power packs, for living life with God.

Fasting is one of the primary practices that can help us to restore the body to its proper place in our efforts to live this embodied life in God's kingdom. Now that we are more than halfway through Lent, I don't expect that any readers will decide to pick up fasting as a Lenten discipline now if they hadn't already done so. But if there is any way in which fasting is beginning to seem inviting to you, we have a day coming which is as appropriate as any to find ways to deny ourselves through fasting: Good Friday. Perhaps you'll want to pause now and prayerfully think about how you will observe that day this year.

A Prayer for the Day:
Lord God, almighty and everlasting Father, you have brought us in safety to this new day: Preserve us with your mighty power, that we may not fall into sin, nor be overcome by adversity; and in all we do, direct us to the fulfilling of your purpose; through Jesus Christ our Lord. Amen.

A Prayer for the Week:
Almighty God, you alone can bring into order the unruly wills and affections of sinners: Grant your people grace to love what you command and desire what you promise; that, among the swift and varied changes of the world, our hearts may surely there be fixed where true joys are to be found; through Jesus Christ our Lord, who lives and reigns with you and the Holy Spirit, one God, now and for ever. Amen.

Day 26: Thursday

Fasting in the Method of the Methodists

In Scot McKnight's book, *Fasting*, which I talked about yesterday, he repeatedly mentions Methodism's founder, John Wesley, because of the central place that fasting had in Wesley's life and in what he taught to the early Methodists. In the book, McKnight says:

The great preacher John Wesley made an observation about fasting that reminds of how customary fasting was in a former era: "While we were at Oxford the rule of every Methodist was (unless in case of sickness) to fast every Wednesday and Friday in the year, in imitation of the primitive church, for which they had the highest reverence." But fasting among the Methodists began to shift noticeably even as Wesley aged.

"And I fear there are now thousands of Methodists, so called, both in England and Ireland, who, following the same bad example, have entirely left off fasting; who are so far from fasting twice a week (as all the stricter Pharisees did) that they do not fast twice in the month. Yea, are there not some of you who do not fast one day, from the beginning of the year to the end?"

And he cut the Methodists of his day no slack because fasting was for Wesley symbolic of spirituality itself:

> "Since, according to this, the man that never fasts is no more in the way to heaven than the man that never prays."[30]

Ouch. (If you're a Methodist reading this, please direct any complaint emails to your founder, not to me.) Even though it's uncomfortable to say, and difficult to believe in today's Methodism, there is no way that anyone can call themselves a Methodist (in any meaningful sense that has an ongoing connection to what it meant to be a Methodist in the movement's beginnings) if fasting in some form is not a regular part of how they shape their lives with God. So, if you aren't a Methodist, but have some Methodist friends, feel free to go quiz them on their fasting habits.

In John Wesley's sermon on the passage which we are looking at this week, when Jesus said, "When you fast…," Wesley observed, "Of all the means of grace there is scarce any concerning which men have run into greater extremes, than…religious fasting. How have some exalted this beyond all scripture and reason; — and others utterly disregarded it."[31]

Wesley urged his Methodists to be part of neither of those extremes, but rather (as he did with so many aspects of the Christian life) to find the wisdom of the way in between them. To aid his people in trying to accomplish this, he gave them sound, practical guidance on fasting, which is still very valuable to us today.

Wesley wanted to practice fasting as it was represented in the Bible and in the majority of Christian history. Though he recognized that fasts of different kinds occurred in scripture, he saw the normal fast as abstaining from food for one day. As McKnight mentioned above, early in Wesley's life, he and the

Day 26: Thursday

Methodists practiced fasting twice per week, on Wednesdays and Fridays. Later, the teaching was reduced to once per week, on all Fridays.

Wesley's own regular practice was to begin his fast on Thursday after supper. This was a weekly way of connecting with Jesus' experience in the Garden of Gethsemane. He would then end his fast on Friday afternoon, to mark the time of Jesus death on the cross, when he said, "It is finished!" (Wesley allowed himself to take liquids during the fast, and taught the Methodists to do so as well.)[32]

Wesley countered one extreme (those who had "utterly disregarded" fasting) by making it a central practice in his own life and in the method he taught to the early Methodists. He countered the other extreme (those who had "exalted this beyond all scripture and reason") by making room for other kinds of fasting–particularly in being careful to never value fasting above one's health. As one alternative to the normal, no food, fast, Wesley suggested what he called "abstinence," which meant that someone would abstain from all foods except those necessary to their health. Another option, which it appears Wesley himself practiced and taught–at least later in his life–was to forego all kinds of "pleasant" foods during the fast.

Whatever the details of it, and whatever the frequency, if we want to find a method of life with God that has similar effects in moving us toward God as experienced by Wesley and his early Methodists, it is certain that he would insist that our routines include fasting.

As I said yesterday, perhaps a good place for us to start is in thinking ahead toward Good Friday. What will

Follow

be a natural, whole-person, *method*ical way for you to respond to all that Good Friday represents?

A Prayer for the Day:

Heavenly Father, in you we live and move and have our being: We humbly pray you so to guide and govern us by your Holy Spirit, that in all the cares and occupations of our life we may not forget you, but may remember that we are ever walking in your sight; through Jesus Christ our Lord. Amen.

A Prayer for the Week:

Almighty God, you alone can bring into order the unruly wills and affections of sinners: Grant your people grace to love what you command and desire what you promise; that, among the swift and varied changes of the world, our hearts may surely there be fixed where true joys are to be found; through Jesus Christ our Lord, who lives and reigns with you and the Holy Spirit, one God, now and for ever. Amen.

Day 27: Friday

Wesley's Sermon and Chilcote's Prayer

One of my favorite books to use for prayer is also one of my favorites for getting to know John Wesley and early Methodism. Paul Chilcote has written a book, titled *Praying in the Wesleyan Spirit: 52 Prayers for Today*, which takes each of Wesley's standard sermons and turns them into 2-3 page prayers. They are very useful for giving shape to our prayers and very helpful in communicating the beliefs and practices that gave rise to early Methodism (which–in my biased opinion–can be beneficial for Christians from any tradition).

In the context of this week's discussion on fasting, I was reminded of how helpful I have found Chilcote's prayer-adaptation of Wesley's sermon on the passage we're considering this week, when Jesus said, "When you fast….":

Blessed God,

Your witness to us in scripture is filled with allusions to fasting, and I know that this spiritual discipline is closely connected to prayer.

I know that fasting is much more than simply abstaining from food for one day or parts of days or on special days. Fasting is an attitude, a discipline of the spirit; it has to do with my longing to be closer to you, my dearest friend.

When I am overwhelmed by sorrow because of the hurtfulness of my words and actions, fasting can be the food for my healing.

When I have fallen into a pattern of overeating and have harmed my own health because of it, fasting can remind me that food is a gift and my body, your temple.

When foolish and hurtful desires well up within me, fasting can refocus my energies and my life on what is truly noble.

When I have abused your good gifts of any kind, fasting can restore a proper perspective toward your many blessings in my life.

When I am struggling in my life of prayer, fasting can draw me closer to you in my efforts to share my deepest longings and my heartfelt desires.

When I need to hear your voice, your corrective as well as your comforting words, fasting can open my ears to your still, small voice within.

When, in the midst of my blindness, you offer me a precious treasure to lift my soul, fasting can open my eyes to perceive your blessed presence in all things.

Certainly, it is important for me to fast, as it were, from sin, from pride, vanity, foolishness, and anger, but you also call me to discipline my spirit by self-denial, so that these unholy attitudes and actions cannot take root in my soul.

Teach me then, O Lord, how to fast in a proper way that will enable your loving spirit to shape and guide my life. Keep my heart and mind focused on you at all times. Remind me that fasting is a means to an end, not an end in itself. Enable me to be attentive to the inward and spiritual

Day 27: Friday

gift. Guard me from extremes that drive love out of my efforts to draw closer to you. Empower me to pray much and to translate my self-discipline into acts of kindness and mercy to others.

When I fast, O Lord, come to me in all the fullness of your love. Change my heart; clean up my life; conform me completely to your will and to your way; make me zealous to glorify you and offer myself up to you anew for your service. Above all else, make me more loving. Amen.[33]

A Prayer for the Day:
Almighty God, whose most dear Son went not up to joy but first he suffered pain, and entered not into glory before he was crucified: Mercifully grant that we, walking in the way of the cross, may find it none other than the way of life and peace; through Jesus Christ our Lord. Amen.

A Prayer for the Week:
Almighty God, you alone can bring into order the unruly wills and affections of sinners: Grant your people grace to love what you command and desire what you promise; that, among the swift and varied changes of the world, our hearts may surely there be fixed where true joys are to be found; through Jesus Christ our Lord, who lives and reigns with you and the Holy Spirit, one God, now and for ever. Amen.

Day 28: Saturday

A Kind of Fasting You Might Need More Than Fasting from Food

A large part of the reason that Christians throughout history have continued to follow Jesus' instructions when he said, "When you fast...," is that fasting can have the effect of increasing our ability to pay attention to God. In groups I lead that follow James Bryan Smith's Apprentice Series[34], we practice a kind of fasting that has nothing to do with food: a 48-hour media fast. I've heard Smith explain this by saying that in generations past, fasting from food was one of the most effective ways that Christians could train themselves to deal with the things that distract us from God. Today, however, our options for distraction have multiplied so dramatically that fasting from food may not be the best place for many of us to start, but instead he gives the suggestion of a 48-hour fast from media.

Here is part of his description of the exercise:

This week I am asking you to consider fasting from all media for two days. This will be challenging, but don't be alarmed: so far no one has died from it. The forty-eight-hour media fast includes

- *the internet*
- *television*
- *newspapers and magazines*
- *radio stations*
- *video games*
- *iPods, mp3 players and stereos*

What will you do with your time? How will you entertain yourself? Try playing a board game or card game with your friends. Read a book...Take a walk, get coffee with friends, exercise. You are beginning to change your mind, which has been filled with false narratives about who you are and what life is about. For forty-eight hours free your mind from the junk; give some space to the Holy Spirit to renew your thinking. This is your way of saying, "I am not under the dominion of the media. I am going to show that I can live without it."[35]

I think he's on to something that is profoundly wise. Some of us may have attempted "normal" fasting (from food), considered ourselves to have failed at it, and given up on it. There could be a variety of reasons for this. For much of my own life, one reason has been that I've eaten so badly and been so addicted to unhealthy foods that fasting was a more intense fight against the addiction than I could handle. Whether or not that is also the case for you, perhaps another place to start is to do what Smith suggests and free ourselves from the noise of all of the kinds of media that constantly surround us. That opens up space for God to work in us, which is the goal of any kind of fasting–or any kind of spiritual practice.

Again, as we have already done a couple of times this week, I invite you to consider this kind of fasting as you look ahead to Good Friday. How will you want to shape your life that day? From which things will you want to free yourself so that you can give your attention more fully to God?

A Prayer for the Day:

Almighty God, who after the creation of the world rested from all your works and sanctified a day of rest for all your creatures: Grant that we, putting away all earthly anxieties, may be duly prepared for the service of your sanctuary, and that our rest here upon earth may be a preparation for the eternal rest promised to your people in heaven; through Jesus Christ our Lord. Amen.

A Prayer for the Week:

Almighty God, you alone can bring into order the unruly wills and affections of sinners: Grant your people grace to love what you command and desire what you promise; that, among the swift and varied changes of the world, our hearts may surely there be fixed where true joys are to be found; through Jesus Christ our Lord, who lives and reigns with you and the Holy Spirit, one God, now and for ever. Amen.

Day 29: Monday

A Road Map for Returning to God

Having tried to lay a good foundation by this point of what Lent is, including spending time the past three weeks in three practices that have long been central to Christians during this season, we turn a corner this week. Now, as one final preparation for Holy Week, we take a step-by-step look at how to do what Lent ultimately invites us to do: return to God. At this point in his story, Jesus is resolutely headed toward his death in Jerusalem. Hopefully, by this point in Lent, we are resolutely denying ourselves, taking up our crosses, and following him.

I'll be borrowing the framework for much of this week's writings from Dallas Willard's landmark book, *Renovation of the Heart*. In that book, he brilliantly describes the parts of a human person and how we can go about resubmitting each of them to be transformed by God. In the course of about one page, he sets out the following two lists, and any of us could spend the rest of our lives working out their implications.

After identifying the parts of a person (which we will spend the remainder of this week exploring) he says that in life away from God, our lives function in this order[36]:

- Body
- Soul
- Mind (Thoughts/Feelings)
- Spirit
- God

In other words, when we live apart from God, it is practically inevitable that our bodies become our main concern. If you don't believe me, scan the headlines in the magazine rack of the checkout aisle the next time you're in the grocery store. Everything focuses on our bodies–how they look, how they feel, how to get more pleasure out of them–basically, a million and one ways for our bodies to make us happier. Jesus made the same observation as he was midway through the Sermon on the Mount, noting that it is natural for the Gentiles (those who know nothing about God or his ways) to be preoccupied with what they eat, what they drink, and what they wear–to live lives centered on their bodies rather than God's kingdom.

In life apart from God, every other part of who we are serves our bodies. Our souls (the "operating system" of our lives, where most things happen at a level deeper than our awareness) orient themselves around serving our bodies. Our minds (our thoughts and our feelings) fall in line, focusing on our bodies. Our spirits (our hearts/our wills/the parts of us that decide) follow suit, making decisions to please our bodies. Then, finally, in life apart from God, God himself is only useful as he can add something that ultimately brings us bodily pleasure. Maybe God can get us a nicer house and a safe and comfortable life, or perhaps he'll reverse all of the bad choices I've made over decades about the things I do with my body (even while I continue in them), or surely

Day 29: Monday

at least I can expect him to keep me out of anything painful. (Yes, we undoubtedly have our "Christianized" versions of the grocery store checkout magazine headlines.)

This is what Paul described as "the mind set on the flesh [which] is death" (See Romans 8:5-7). Life, ultimately, does not work this way, which is precisely why God wants something else for us.

One of the best, very biblical, definitions of holiness is "a way of life that works," and Dallas identifies the order of a life under God (a holy life) like this[37]:

- God
- Spirit
- Mind
- Soul
- Body

In this order, the body is still not bad, but rather than being the focus of everything it becomes our ally, the vehicle through which all other aspects of our lives with God can take place, which is precisely why we should properly care for it. "The body serves the soul; the soul, the mind; the mind, the spirit; and the spirit, God....The life 'from above' flows from God throughout the whole person."[38] God is in God's proper place, rather than the body being there. (Remember all of those warnings in the Bible about idolatry?) Then, the door is opened for us to *actually become* people who love God with all of our heart, soul, mind, and strength. This is the way that Paul describes as "life and peace."

"Okay, now that we have all of *that* figured out..." No, you don't, and neither do I. But we have a wealth of guidance available to us on how we can proceed. We will spend the remainder of our week being specific and practical about how we can, *really*, move our lives toward God and experience more of the goodness of a way of life that works.

A Prayer for the Day:
O God, the King eternal, whose light divides the day from the night and turns the shadow of death into the morning: Drive far from us all wrong desires, incline our hearts to keep your law, and guide our feet into the way of peace; that, having done your will with cheerfulness while it was day, we may, when night comes, rejoice to give you thanks; through Jesus Christ our Lord. Amen.

A Prayer for the Week:
Almighty and everliving God, in your tender love for the human race you sent your Son our Savior Jesus Christ to take upon him our nature, and to suffer death upon the cross, giving us the example of his great humility: Mercifully grant that we may walk in the way of his suffering, and also share in his resurrection; through Jesus Christ our Lord, who lives and reigns with you and the Holy Spirit, one God, for ever and ever. Amen.

Day 30: Tuesday

Returning to God with Our Minds

If we are going to fully return to God–as individuals, families, churches, communities, and beyond–*the* place that change will begin is in our thoughts. Though that might sound simple enough, we normally don't act as if it is true. Think of how many times someone has tried to urge you to change something, not by altering the way you think about it, but by some other means–primarily our emotions and our wills. Though innumerable attempts are made at guilting us into things, or getting us to grit our teeth and just try harder, neither of those are sufficient for lasting change. (If this is too abstract, just think about the last time someone tried to convince you to do something solely by saying you don't do that thing enough–whether exercise, buying jewelry, going to church, saving for your retirement, or anything else. Even if you've acted on one of those appeals in the past, did the behavior last for you?)

Tomorrow we'll discuss why the appeals to our willpower don't work, but since we're approaching this week's theme of returning to God in a step-by-step manner, we can never underestimate the primary power of what we put into our minds. In *Renovation of the Heart* (which provides the framework for all of this week's reflections), Dallas Willard says, "The ultimate freedom we have as human beings is the power to select what we will allow or require our minds to dwell upon."[39] He also says, "Thoughts are the place where we can and must begin to change."[40]

Why is this the case? Because our lives inevitably follow the course of what we think about. We live at the mercy of the stories, images, and ideas that fill our minds. They affect *everything* about the kind of person we are becoming. And, as Dallas said, we have tremendous freedom in selecting the things that we allow into our minds and what our minds will dwell upon.

To make this a bit less theoretical, hopefully a recent experience of my own can help you make a connection with similar ways that your thinking affects the entirety of your life:

I recently had a stretch of seven business days, six of which contained some medical test, procedure, or minor surgery. Everything ended up just fine, but even though my attitude was very positive when the appointments began, I had about a day and a half when my resolve had worn down and my attitude crashed. It seemed like every test kept leading to something else to be done, and suddenly a multitude of "what ifs" bombarded me. Rather than redirecting my mind to other things, which would have been the wise and more sensible thing to do, I let my mind dwell on the "what ifs," and fear began to sink its claws in. "What if…my wife…? What if…my kids…? What if…our income…?" While the what ifs and their accompanying fear were bouncing around in my mind, I found myself being anxious (which I'm usually not), impatient with others (which I am too often, but

Day 30: Tuesday

have made good strides in learning to avoid), and unmotivated by things that are normally very life-giving to me.

Thankfully, I was fresh off of a good discussion in my Apprentice Group about worry and how, in God's kingdom, we *can* actually learn to live without it. So, even though more of my mental energy than normal was going toward worry, I was aware–with good information still fresh in my mind–of what was going on and was able to counter it. I am very grateful that one of the things we do in those Apprentice Groups is to memorize chunks of scripture–not just an isolated verse or two, but long passages. With those passages stored in my mind, I was eventually able to redirect my mind to them rather than to my worries. When my mind was occupied in more positive ways, the fear and anxiety subsided and I began again to enjoy the people and activities that are such gracious gifts in my life.

Hopefully you can relate. Our emotions follow our thoughts. Then we make decisions largely based on those emotions. We then enact those decisions in physical ways (some of which we're aware and some we are not), which inevitably affect others around us. All of this, over the months, years, and decades of our lifetimes adds up to a soul that is either able to live well with God, itself, and others, or one that is not.

Dallas often made the point that each of us is already in the process of becoming the kind of person we will be forever.[41] That's true, and of all the things we'll talk about this week that we can do as part of our road map for returning to God, today's is the most foundational: everything about who we are begins to move in a Godward direction, or away from God, beginning with what we put into our minds and what we allow them to dwell on.

Consider these:

- "What are three 'thoughts' that have occupied your mind this week? Why those thoughts, and not some others? What have their effects on your life been?"[42]
- Begin to train your mind to dwell on God more often by slowly memorizing a passage of scripture, such as Colossians 3:1-17, Psalm 23, John 14:1-27, or Romans 8:1-15. (I know what you're thinking, but yes, you can do it. God will help.)
- Or, find a time this week to read through one of the gospels (Matthew, Mark, Luke or John) in one or two sittings. If you're crunched for time, Mark is the shortest–you can probably read it in about an hour and a half or less.

A Prayer for the Day:
O God, the author of peace and lover of concord, to know you is eternal life and to serve you is perfect freedom: Defend us, your humble servants, in all assaults of our enemies; that we, surely trusting in your defense, may not fear the power of any adversaries; through the might of Jesus Christ our Lord. Amen.

A Prayer for the Week:
Almighty and everliving God, in your tender love for the human race you sent your Son our Savior Jesus Christ to take upon him our nature, and to suffer death upon the cross, giving us the example of his great humility: Mercifully grant that we may walk in the way of his suffering, and also share in his resurrection; through Jesus Christ our Lord, who lives and reigns with you and the Holy Spirit, one God, for ever and ever. Amen.

Day 31: Wednesday

Returning to God with Our Hearts

What I'm about to say may not make me popular with some, but here goes: I'll admit that I'm a bit gun-shy when we talk in church about doing anything with our "hearts." I think the term gets used far too often, and–perhaps because of nothing more mature than trying to be macho–I always have my radar up for things that are going to require me to do something "touchy-feely." Whenever something shows up as a blip on that screen, I usually try to avoid it, and one of the primary indicators to me that I might want to avoid something in church is if its title includes the word "heart." (If, in addition to the word, there is also any sort of heart-shaped clip art, I will almost certainly steer clear.)

I'm not proud of this, and I realize that it's not a particularly holy tendency, but at least I'm being honest.

So I admit that machismo rather than maturity is mostly to blame for my anti-heart reaction, but I think there's also another level to it: usually we have very little sense of what we're talking about in church when we talk about doing things with the heart. Most of our associations with it have to do with our feelings or emotions (which explains my avoidance of anything pointing in that direction), so any suggestion that we should do things such as praying with our hearts, or reading the Bible with our hearts, or even loving God with our hearts meets my initial defenses.

Again, thanks to Dallas Willard's work in *Renovation of the Heart*, I've come to see that loving, reading, and praying with our hearts are all things that should have a very concrete, practical meaning. In the book, Dallas proposes that–according to the images in the scriptures–talking about doing something with our hearts isn't actually talking about our feelings or emotions, but rather about our wills (to which the macho me heaves a sigh of relief).

Dallas makes the case that references in the scriptures to the heart, the spirit, and the will are all referring to the same part of us, essentially the part of us that chooses.[43] Regardless of whether or not you share my disinclinations toward the touchy-feely, this is actually very good news for all of us. I'll see if I can explain why.

Think for a moment of someone who, in your estimation, is "world-class" at something, perhaps a professional athlete, musician, or some other kind of performer. We normally think of such people as not only being talented, but also having tremendous willpower. They have made the difficult decisions, day after day and year after year, which have resulted in their world-class abilities.

But what if I told you that I know something surprising about whichever great performer you have in mind: that, rather than having tremendous willpower, they actually have *none at all*? What if I told you that neither do I, and neither do you?

This makes sense if, instead of thinking of the heart as something indefinite but related to our feelings, we think

Day 31: Wednesday

of the heart in the context of a human life as we're considering it this week (again, thanks to Dallas). If we look at the heart/spirit/will as the part of us that chooses, and we understand the ground we covered yesterday about the role that our minds play in shaping everything about who we are, we can let ourselves off the hook about not having enough willpower to do certain things, because we'll realize that the will actually has no power. Instead, it is pointed in some direction(s), and makes decisions accordingly.

Back to your world-class performers: It's undeniably true that they indeed have made the tough decisions over years and decades to refine their talents into world-class abilities. But if what I'm saying is true, they didn't make those decisions based on tremendous willpower. Rather, they put the right things into their minds, and directed their minds to dwell on those things, so that whenever big or small decisions were presented to them, their hearts/wills/spirits chose accordingly, and all of those choices added up over time to turn (naturally) into remarkable abilities.

So here comes the good news: the ability we are after is the ability to live our lives according to God's desires for us, namely that we would be people with the character of Jesus who participate in his kingdom in our everyday lives. *This does not rest on our willpower.* More concretely: your ability (or lack thereof) to actually live without anger, lust, deception, vanity, greed, and worry–to bless those who curse you and be completely free of the need to judge others–does not depend upon you having a world-class amount of willpower. No one does. We're all off the willpower hook.

What does matter, tremendously, if we seriously want to return to God with our hearts, is that *we do the things that will naturally—over the course of months, years, and decades—point our hearts/wills/spirits to choose in the direction of that kind of life.*

So, if you want to live a life completely in God's will five years from now, the question is not whether you have a five-year strategic plan to get you there. The question is whether, today, you are putting the things in your mind that will shape your thoughts and feelings in such a way that, when decision times come over the next five years, you will consistently choose in that Godward direction. And—the biggest surprise is—rather than requiring tremendous willpower, *it won't even be difficult.*[44] (See Matthew 11:28-29.)

A Prayer for the Day:
Lord God, almighty and everlasting Father, you have brought us in safety to this new day: Preserve us with your mighty power, that we may not fall into sin, nor be overcome by adversity; and in all we do, direct us to the fulfilling of your purpose; through Jesus Christ our Lord. Amen.

A Prayer for the Week:
Almighty and everliving God, in your tender love for the human race you sent your Son our Savior Jesus Christ to take upon him our nature, and to suffer death upon the cross, giving us the example of his great humility: Mercifully grant that we may walk in the way of his suffering, and also share in his resurrection; through Jesus Christ our Lord, who lives and reigns with you and the Holy Spirit, one God, for ever and ever. Amen.

Day 32: Thursday

Returning to God with Our Bodies

When you and I look in the mirror, we see the primary tool that God has given us to know and serve him. We have covered some of this ground in previous weeks, but it is worth revisiting since, as Dallas Willard says, the role of the body in the spiritual life is "the least understood aspect of progress in Christlikeness."[45] Your body is not the enemy in your attempts to live life with God. Instead, it is a marvelous vehicle for loving God and loving others, and it is the only instrument God has given us to do so.

But…you and I know our bodies well. We know that they fail us. Jesus' statement to Peter, James, and John on his last night with them sounds truer than what I wrote in the previous paragraph: "The spirit is willing, but the flesh is weak." We know too well the temptations that are ever present in our bodies, as they seem to unceasingly pull us toward gluttony, greed, lust, vanity, and all-around superficial living. Isn't the "spiritual" life about learning how to effectively ignore our bodies so that we can get on with the really important things God wants of us? And, at the end of it all, isn't the point that we finally become free of these bodies, leave them behind, and go on to live the ultimate spiritual life forever with God in heaven?

That has been a prevalent viewpoint of many Christians for a long time, but scripture and the best of Christian tradition answer with a resounding "no." Our bodies are the height of God's good creation, and if our lives with God in this age are ever to make sense, we must come to grips with the essential role they play in enabling us to become the kind of people that God wants us to be forever.

Though the importance and worth of our bodies is communicated throughout the Bible, it is nowhere stated more emphatically than in the passages dealing with Jesus' resurrection. To see how well your theology on this issue matches up with what the Bible says, notice your reaction to this statement: *Jesus **never left his body** behind*. We know that the story says his tomb was empty. He never left his body behind. What this means is that there is *still* an *embodied* Jesus ruling as the anointed King of the world. What happened to him (being raised in his own real body–though it was different in some ways) will also happen to everyone. Our bodies really matter, and they always will, as the future that awaits us is just as embodied as the life we know now–only, in some very good sense, more so. (Is your thinking being stirred yet?)

So, in the context of this Lent and our discussion this week about returning to God, what difference does that make for the lives that we are really living in these bodies today? Willard again:

Our part in this transformation, in addition to constant faith and hope in Christ, is purposeful, strategic use of our bodies in ways which will retrain them, replacing "the motions of sin in our members" with the motions of Christ. This is how we take up our cross daily. It is how we submit our bodies a living sacrifice, how we "offer the parts of our body to him as instruments of righteousness." (Rom 6:13)[46]

In other words, the bodily habits which pull us away from God are not just in our imaginations, but they are real, ingrained, bodily habits that need to be dealt with. More than dealt with–they need to be "killed off," "crucified with Christ," as we replace them with habits that are conducive to God's life in us rather than opposed to it.

It is progress for us to realize that the things that block God's life in us are always bodily, whether in an obvious case like sexual lust, or in a less obvious example such as gossip. (How many times has your *mouth* said something before you realized what you were doing?) Yet even when we accept that, how do we deal with those things? If a main bodily stumbling block for me is overeating and finding my comfort in food rather than in God, how do I employ my body in the opposite direction?

The answer has to do with something we can call indirection. We don't defeat greed by trying really hard not to be greedy. We don't kill off the embodied habits that cut us off from God's life by just trying to do their opposites. No, we put other bodily habits in place (such as giving, praying, and fasting–or others like reflecting on the scriptures, solitude, worship, fellowship, etc.) which open us up, piece by piece, to God's grace. There is more grace than we can imagine and when we open ourselves to it through these means that have been passed down to us, our bodies become places where God dwells, and he deals with our sinful habits over time.

In light of what we've already looked at this week, this can only happen over the long haul when,
- first–our *minds* have been filled with the things that lead us to think about God as he really is, then our emotions become characterized by love, joy, and peace rather than hurry and worry;
- then–that part of us that chooses, the *heart/spirit/will*, naturally–even easily–chooses things that lead us in a Godward direction;
- and then–as a matter of course, every one of those choices will be empowered by these *bodies* that we live in. This is true regardless of how they look, how old or young they are, and what medical issues they might be facing.

So, what is one way that you already know to "present your body to God as a living sacrifice" today?

A Prayer for the Day:
Heavenly Father, in you we live and move and have our being: We humbly pray you so to guide and govern us by your Holy Spirit, that in all the cares and occupations of our life we may not forget you, but may remember that we are ever walking in your sight; through Jesus Christ our Lord. Amen.

A Prayer for the Week:
Almighty and everliving God, in your tender love for the human race you sent your Son our Savior Jesus Christ to take upon him our nature, and to suffer death upon the cross, giving us the example of his great humility: Mercifully grant that we may walk in the way of his suffering, and also share in his resurrection; through Jesus Christ our Lord, who lives and reigns with you and the Holy Spirit, one God, for ever and ever. Amen.

Day 33: Friday

Returning to God with Our Relationships

Though we have all probably heard people adamantly say otherwise, there is nothing that is actually "just between you and God." Everything about our lives with God inevitably affects others. Plus, as inescapably social beings, our lives with God are always affected by others. So, in the context of this week's discussions, talking about returning to God with our relationships is a bit of a chicken-and-egg discussion. Our relationships play a huge role in shaping the quality of our life with God, and the quality of our life with God shapes every relationship we have.

Let's look first at the way that our relationships impact our life with God: We do not become spiritually healthy people apart from a spiritually healthy community. John Wesley was perhaps (in my biased opinion) as effective as anyone in Christian history at helping individuals grow, and he insisted that we do not progress in life with God on our own. He said, "'Holy solitaries' is a phrase no more consistent with the gospel than holy adulterers. The gospel of Christ knows of no religion but social; no holiness but social holiness."[47]

The application here is downright simple: if you want to be someone who has more of the character of Jesus, spend more time with more people who have more of the character of Jesus.

So what about the other side of it–thinking that things are just between God and me? Wesley says, "Christianity is essentially a social religion...to turn it into a solitary one is to destroy it."[48] Part of Jesus' point in saying that his hearers were a city on a hill that cannot be hidden is this inevitability of our lives affecting those around us. I would not want to try to hide New York City. It is just as difficult to keep anything between just God and me.

Some considerations for each side of this:
- When I look back at the path of my Christian life, a major turning point was when, before my senior year of college, I sent a letter to my campus pastor. He was the most authentic disciple of Jesus I knew, and I wanted his kind of life with God. I had no idea what his schedule was like, but I asked if we could spend some time together. He invited me to be with him for an hour every week, and the course of my life changed. Think of someone whose life with God is of the kind that you desire to have. Invite them to a meal, send them an email, or give them a call.
- Is there some area of your life where you'd prefer to think something was remaining between you and God and not affecting anyone else? If what I have said here is true, who might it be affecting without you having been aware? What do you need to do about it?

Day 33: Friday

A Prayer for the Day:

Almighty God, whose most dear Son went not up to joy but first he suffered pain, and entered not into glory before he was crucified: Mercifully grant that we, walking in the way of the cross, may find it none other than the way of life and peace; through Jesus Christ our Lord. Amen.

A Prayer for the Week:

Almighty and everliving God, in your tender love for the human race you sent your Son our Savior Jesus Christ to take upon him our nature, and to suffer death upon the cross, giving us the example of his great humility: Mercifully grant that we may walk in the way of his suffering, and also share in his resurrection; through Jesus Christ our Lord, who lives and reigns with you and the Holy Spirit, one God, for ever and ever. Amen.

Day 34: Saturday

Returning to God with Our Souls

This week's reflections have tried to form something of a roadmap for how we can return to God in an authentic and thorough way, for the remainder of our lives. When all of these pieces (our minds, hearts/spirits/wills, bodies, and relationships) are headed in the same Godward direction together, our souls will also find themselves whole in the kind of life God intended us to live.

We have immense trouble today acknowledging that we have souls, and even when we do–having any clue what they are or what to do about them. Since this week's framework has largely come from Dallas Willard's book, *Renovation of the Heart*, and his description of the soul is about the only one that has ever made much sense to me, allow me to quote a couple of paragraphs:

What is running your life at any given moment is your soul. Not external circumstances, or your thoughts, or your intentions, or even your feelings, but your soul. The soul is that aspect of your whole being that correlates, integrates, and enlivens everything going on in the various dimensions of the self. It is the life-center of the human being. It regulates whatever is occurring in each of those dimensions and how they interact with each other and respond to surrounding events in the overall governance of your life. The soul is "deep" in the sense of being basic or foundational and also in the sense that it lies almost totally beyond conscious awareness.

In the person with the "well-kept heart," the soul will be itself properly ordered under God and in harmony with reality. The outcome will be…"a person who is prepared for and capable of responding to the situations of life in ways that are good and right." For such a person, the human spirit will be in correct relationship to God. With his assisting grace, it will bring the soul into subjection to God and the mind (thoughts, feelings) into subjection to the soul. The social context and the body will then come into subjection to thoughts and feelings that are in agreement with truth and with God's intent and purposes for us. Any given event in our life would then proceed as it should, because our soul is functioning properly under God.[49]

In another place, Dallas compares the soul to something like the operating system on your computer.[50] We never notice the large majority of what happens there, though it is the regulator of everything we experience. Our operating systems and our souls normally only receive attention when something goes badly wrong with them. So how do we direct our souls in our desire to return to God?

We have to clear out space in our lives for God's grace to work at the soul level, deeper than our feelings. The two primary practices the church has hung on to through the ages for doing this are silence and solitude. We all need these, regardless of whether we are introverts or extroverts, because otherwise we will drown out anything that may be happening at that level—more often than not, with good things.

If we want our entire lives to return to God this Lent and beyond, we cannot do without time in quiet, apart from other people, for the simple purpose of being with God. Wesley urged his early Methodists to retire from the world at least each morning and evening to be alone with God, saying that if we spend an entire day in constant interactions with others, our souls will surely be damaged.[51]

So now that we've come to the brink of Holy Week, how is your soul? Is it well-kept and prepared to follow Jesus through the next week? Or is it so accustomed to being ignored that you might avoid giving it any space to be with God, even during this most sacred of times?

A Prayer for the Day:
Almighty God, who after the creation of the world rested from all your works and sanctified a day of rest for all your creatures: Grant that we, putting away all earthly anxieties, may be duly prepared for the service of your sanctuary, and that our rest here upon earth may be a preparation for the eternal rest promised to your people in heaven; through Jesus Christ our Lord. Amen.

A Prayer for the Week:
Almighty and everliving God, in your tender love for the human race you sent your Son our Savior Jesus Christ to take upon him our nature, and to suffer death upon the cross, giving us the example of his great humility: Mercifully grant that we may walk in the way of his suffering, and also share in his resurrection; through Jesus Christ our Lord, who lives and reigns with you and the Holy Spirit, one God, for ever and ever. Amen.

Day 35

Monday in Holy Week

We have come to the most widely-known eight days in all of human history, called Holy Week by Christians. It began yesterday, Palm Sunday, as we remembered the story of Jesus riding into Jerusalem to the crowds cheering as if they were welcoming a king, and it will continue on through Jesus' last night with his disciples, his arrest and mock trial, his crucifixion, death and burial. And then his resurrection will change everything, for everyone, forever.

We are familiar with Palm Sunday, Maundy Thursday, Good Friday, and Easter Sunday (or if not, you soon will be), but what about the other days? What took place on the day after Jesus' royal entry into Jerusalem? And on Tuesday, Wednesday, and Saturday?

This week, we will try to walk day by day through the events of the corresponding days of Jesus' life. Matthew, Mark, Luke and John were not particularly concerned with telling their stories in a way that would allow us to put together a nice, exact historical reconstruction of exactly what happened at each point during the week. That's fine because those aren't the most important pieces. They were rightly more focused on getting their points about Jesus across than they were about trivia games we might like to play centuries later about what happened on which day. Nonetheless, we can still put

Follow

together a plausible sequence of events for the week, and doing so is our goal as we continue in this journey of denying ourselves, taking up our crosses, and following our Lord.

So for today, Monday in Holy Week:

According to Mark's telling, after Jesus entered Jerusalem to the shouts of the crowds, he went to the temple courts. Since it was already late in the day, he went to stay the night in Bethany with the twelve before returning to the temple the next morning (presumably, Monday).

On their way to the temple, Jesus approached a fig tree but did not find any fruit on it. Then came one of the scenes which I am sure I will never see painted on the wall of a children's Sunday School classroom.

In the ways that we typically think of Jesus, we would likely expect his reaction to finding no fruit on the fig tree to be something like one of the following:

- Maybe he would look at the tree, have a tear well up in his eye while a bluebird comes and lands on his shoulder to tweet a song in a minor key over Jesus' sadness that this tree had not been able to properly produce its fruit. Jesus could have meekly mourned over the sad tree.
- Or, perhaps Jesus would just look intently at the tree, command it to produce some fruit, and it would instantly have jumbo, juicy figs for all of the disciples to share. Jesus could have powerfully, victoriously healed the unfruitful tree.

But Jesus did neither of those things. Instead of mourning over the tree or healing it, he *cursed* it: "May no one ever eat fruit from you again."

Day 35: Monday

If I had been one of the twelve, I surely would have stood there thinking, "Ouch, Teacher. Hunger pangs make you a little crabby this morning?"

But, being as capable of a storyteller as Mark was, he didn't allow us to stay there, wondering about the stability of Jesus' emotional state. (If that was the point, and he was that crabby after missing breakfast, what would he have been like after fasting for forty days in the desert?) Instead, he gave us one of his story-sandwiches, where he began one story, moved to another, then came back to the first in order to point out the links between the two.

In this story-sandwich, this incident with the poor little fig tree is the bread, while the meat is what Jesus did when he arrived in the temple.

On reaching Jerusalem, Jesus entered the temple courts and began driving out those who were buying and selling there. He overturned the tables of the money changers and the benches of those selling doves, and would not allow anyone to carry merchandise through the temple courts. And as he taught them, he said, "Is it not written: 'My house will be called a house of prayer for all nations'? But you have made it 'a den of robbers.'"
(Mark 11:15-17, NIV)

So now we have two consecutive stories of Jesus that don't get painted on the walls of children's Sunday School rooms. In order to understand what's happening here, we have to recognize that Jesus was not staging a protest of the commercialization of people's worship in the temple. Perhaps, if Mark hadn't connected the temple story to the fig tree, we might be able to come away with that as the full meaning. Instead, since Jesus' encounter with the fig tree ended in a curse for the tree's failure to be and do what it was created for, Jesus then proceeded to do the same thing in the temple.

The temple existed to symbolize God's dwelling with Israel for the sake of the world, but its leaders had turned it into a place to promote violence toward outsiders and injustice toward Israel's own people. So– just as Jesus' words to the tree stopped its natural processes, his brief but symbolic words and actions in the temple stopped the course of events in the place that was the center of Jewish life.

Mark wraps up the story-sandwich as the disciples return to the city the next morning and pass by the same tree, now withered from the roots. He wants us to get the point: Jesus' action in the temple was a warning that, if it continued failing to be and do what it was created for, the same fate awaited the temple that came to the tree. And to make sure we don't miss the lesson, Mark puts an exclamation point on his story-sandwich through Jesus' comments when Peter noticed that the fig tree Jesus cursed had withered:

"Have faith in God," Jesus answered. "Truly I tell you, if anyone says to this mountain, 'Go, throw yourself into the sea,' and does not doubt in their heart but believes that what they say will happen, it will be done for them. Therefore I tell you, whatever you ask for in prayer, believe that you have received it, and it will be yours. And when you stand praying, if you hold anything against anyone, forgive them, so that your Father in heaven may forgive you your sins."

Again, remember that this is part of the sandwich, rather than a stand-alone teaching. Jesus isn't saying that Peter and the others could also learn to do cool things like wither fruit trees, make mountains move, or anything else that they decide on a prayer-whim. No, the point is still the meat of this story-sandwich: the temple. When Jesus says, "this mountain," I imagine that he also pointed a finger toward the Temple Mount. He's teaching the disciples to pray that God's new order would replace the old and that, inconceivable as it may have seemed to them, the temple was nearing a time when it would be no more.

Jesus' dire warnings about the temple came to pass in 70 AD when the Romans laid siege to Jerusalem, including the temple's destruction.

Also, just as important for our journey through Holy Week is to realize that because of this and Jesus' procession into Jerusalem as a king the previous day, his impending death was now inevitable. No one could ride into Jerusalem as a king and proceed to say and do the things toward the temple which Jesus said and did and be allowed to live. When we read the story in this light, we begin to get the sense that Jesus was not a victim of Roman and Jewish injustice when he died on the cross; rather, he seems to be orchestrating the story exactly as he saw fit.

A Prayer for Monday in Holy Week:
Almighty God, whose dear Son went not up to joy but first he suffered pain, and entered not into glory before he was crucified: Mercifully grant that we, walking in the way of the cross, may find it none other that the way of life and peace; through Jesus Christ your Son our Lord, who lives and reigns with you and the Holy Spirit, one God, for ever and ever. Amen.

Day 36

Tuesday in Holy Week

So far in Holy Week, Jesus has ridden into Jerusalem the way a king would and allowed the crowds to welcome him as one, and then he went straight to the heart of the nation (the temple) and in the strongest words and actions possible, made clear that judgment was coming upon it. With those things having happened, it is not difficult to foresee confrontation coming.

The morning after Jesus briefly–yet powerfully and symbolically–stopped all of the activity in the temple, he returned there. As expected, the confrontation came:

One day as Jesus was teaching the people in the temple courts and proclaiming the good news, the chief priests and the teachers of the law, together with the elders, came up to him. "Tell us by what authority you are doing these things," they said. "Who gave you this authority?"

He replied, "I will also ask you a question. Tell me: John's baptism—was it from heaven, or of human origin?"

They discussed it among themselves and said, "If we say, 'From heaven,' he will ask, 'Why didn't you believe him?' But if we say, 'Of human origin,' all the people will stone us, because they are persuaded that John was a prophet."

So they answered, "We don't know where it was from."

Day 36: Tuesday

> *Jesus said, "Neither will I tell you by what authority I am doing these things."*
> (Luke 20:1-8, NIV)

The authorities' question to Jesus was a natural one. He had been acting like the person in charge–of the temple, of Jerusalem, and therefore of all Israel–but according to the system, he was a nobody. His questioners were the ones who had the positions of power, not him. "By what authority are you doing these things?" is both a question and an accusation, similar to asking, "Just who in the world do you think you are?"

At first glance, Jesus' response about John the Baptist looks like a clever trick question, allowing both sides to avoid answering the other's question, but Jesus was actually providing a clear answer to them. When asked, "Who in the world do you think you are?" Jesus points them back to John the Baptist, whose claim to be the forerunner of the Messiah said plenty about who Jesus was–*if* John really was God's prophet. At another level, by referencing John, Jesus is pointing back to his own baptism at John's hand, when a voice came from heaven and said, "You are my son, whom I love. With you I am well pleased." Jesus was saying, "*That* is who I am, and where I get my authority."[52]

If John the Baptist was a fake, so was Jesus, and the establishment would have had the right to treat him as such. But if John was the real thing, then Jesus clearly had more authority over the temple, Jerusalem, Israel– and the world–than any of the men questioning him.

So we could turn Jesus' response into a statement rather than a question:

> *"Who in the world do you think you are? What kind of authority do you think you have to do things like this?"*

> *"I am the one who came after John, with all that that means."*

Jesus then went on teaching in the temple, continuing to say extremely provocative things about the temple and its leaders. He told stories (in which the parallels were not difficult to draw) about people in power mistreating, even killing, their master's servants. He pointed out their hypocrisy and injustice toward the innocent, and the price that others–like a poor widow giving all she had in an offering–paid for it.

Yes, the temple was beautiful, but if Israel continued to reject God's way, which was being perfectly embodied before them in Jesus, it was inevitable that the temple's destruction was coming. "Not one stone will be left on another."

Of course this was shocking. It was like taking all of our meaningful national sites which we assume will be around forever, and saying, "Every one of these will be turned into ruins–and it will happen while our generation is still here to see it."

The only way to describe something so tumultuous would be to use language that could communicate the earth-shattering nature of the events, like the old prophets did: "the sun will go dark, the moon won't give any light, the stars will fall out of the sky" (see Matthew 24).

Israel was headed on a course for destruction, and if they continued to refuse Jesus' message and change direction (repent), their doom was inevitable. (As we mentioned yesterday–it all happened about 40 years later, and it was indeed as horrible as Jesus described.)

I said yesterday that Jesus' fate was sealed after riding into the city as a king and saying/doing what he said/

did in the temple. Now, after an extra day of saying such provocative things about the temple and its leadership, it was extra-sealed. The authorities would not allow this man to live.

Though those in Jesus' circle must have been aware of the tension and conflict, many of them still didn't grasp what it meant. Still thinking of Jesus as the kind of Messiah they had always expected, they couldn't foresee what was coming for him in a few more days.

At least one woman understood, though. She saw what was happening with clarity. After the intense day in the temple, Jesus and his group returned for the evening to Bethany. While guests in a home, eating dinner with the twelve, this woman came in, approached Jesus, and unreservedly poured very expensive perfume on him, as one would do to a corpse before burying it. She knew what Jesus knew–he was about to die.

Again, as we mentioned yesterday, when we watch this story unfold, it is impossible to look at Jesus as a helpless victim. Rather, in the kind of way he described as "lose your life and you will find it," he seems to be in control of what was happening.

A Prayer for Tuesday in Holy Week:
O God, by the passion of your blessed Son you made an instrument of shameful death to be for us the means of life: Grant us so to glory in the cross of Christ, that we may gladly suffer shame and loss for the sake of your Son our Savior Jesus Christ; who lives and reigns with you and the Holy Spirit, one God, for ever and ever. Amen.

Day 37

Wednesday in Holy Week

I have occasionally met people who have very strange names (like the time in college when I was introduced to two sisters named Rainbow and Sunshine), but one name comes to mind which I've never heard of a parent giving to their child: Judas.

I'm sure there is an exception out there somewhere, and I hope that his parents either weren't English-speaking or just didn't know this story very well, but–thankfully–not many parents choose to give their sons the name of the most well-known traitor in the history of the world.

Despite its history after Jesus, the name, Judas, has strong roots. It was a common name for Jewish boys in Jesus' day. Two of the twelve disciples had the name, plus one of Jesus' brothers. Judas, Jude, Judah–even Jew and Jewish–all come from the same name/word and all point back in Israel's history to one of Jacob's sons. In Jesus' day, it was a heroic name with royal implications. Judas Maccabaeus successfully led a revolt against Israel's oppressors a couple of centuries before Jesus was born. Judas the Galilean led a revolt against the Romans during Jesus' boyhood, which was crushed brutally.

Day 37: Wednesday

But ever since the day we're considering in this reflection, somewhere around Wednesday of the last week of Jesus' life, the name Judas brings to mind evil, darkness, and the worst aspects of the human heart.

Judas was part of the inner circle from the beginning of Jesus' public career. Despite how artwork through the centuries has portrayed him, there was nothing about Judas that made him stand out as the obvious choice for "Most Likely to Betray God's Anointed." He was one of the group, hoping that Jesus was the one for whom they had been waiting. He was there passing baskets around to the crowd when five loaves of bread and two fish had fed thousands of people. He saw the sick healed, demons cast out, and the dead raised to life–perhaps, at Jesus' instruction, even doing some of these things himself just as the other disciples did. He was there when Jesus taught, and could undoubtedly sense that it was like no other teaching he had ever heard.

Though speculation abounds and all kinds of possibilities exist as to why Judas went to the chief priests and asked, "What are you willing to give me if I deliver him over to you?" and then accepted the deal for the price of thirty pieces of silver, we can never know what went on inside of him.

Still, I'll add my own speculation to the mix: perhaps something about the previous few days had convinced Judas that what he had hoped Jesus would accomplish was ultimately not going to happen. Yesterday, we mentioned how–even though the tension in Jesus' interactions in the temple was so high–apparently, most of Jesus' followers still didn't foresee what was coming nor understand the warnings he had given them about it. That is, except for one woman, who showed her understanding by anointing Jesus for his burial while he was sitting at a supper with the twelve.

Maybe, after all, that woman wasn't the only one who understood. Maybe Judas did by that point as well. Or possibly her actions at that dinner and Jesus' response to her were what allowed Judas to see what, by then, was inevitable: this man, whom they had thought was the Messiah–their deliverer–was going to die, and apparently that was even what Jesus had expected for some time. Jesus had spent the last couple of days in the temple picking a fight that he intended to lose.

In the minds of almost everyone who had followed Jesus to that point, realizing the fate that awaited him would have meant that he *could not* have been the one they had hoped him to be. The Messiah (the real one) would deliver, conquer enemies, restore Israel, and rule as king; anyone who would head knowingly into his own defeat and death therefore could not be God's anointed one. It would be impossible to think of anyone executed before coming to power as being the long-awaited king.

We are arrogant to think we would have caught on any more quickly than the rest of the disciples. They simply had no framework for understanding Messiah-ship that looked like what Jesus was about to do. Perhaps that clicked a bit sooner for Judas than it did for the others, and as soon as he realized it, he therefore had to get out. (Surely he realized that if Jesus was going to die, his followers would become targeted as well, and there was no reason to go to the grave with a failed Messiah.)

I don't know how much Jesus knew about Judas when he chose him to be one of the twelve. The gospels seem to be clear that Jesus knew during his time with the disciples that one of them would turn away, and John even says that Jesus knew from the beginning who would betray him.

Regardless of the timing–whether Jesus knew what Judas would do from the first time they laid eyes on one another, or if it was some time after that–considering the relationship between the two of them makes me tremble for a couple of reasons.

First, I realize that I am not so far from Judas as I would like to think. Jesus has utterly disappointed me at times, when I counted on him to do things I thought he said he would do, and then they did not happen. I have never wanted out as Judas did, but I've also had a remarkably easier time of following Jesus than in his case. Of course I like to think that if I was at the Last Supper, I would have been the one reclining close enough to Jesus to whisper a question in his ear, but it's just as likely that I would have been the one who dipped the bread in the bowl with him.

The other part of it that makes me shudder–and want to spend some time on my face before God–is to realize that regardless of when Jesus knew what he knew about Judas, Jesus loved him. Jesus kept him around, shared his life with Judas. He washed Judas' feet. He passed bread to Judas, saying, "Take it. This is my body." Then he passed wine and said, "This is my blood…" Only after all of these things did Jesus tell him, "What you are about to do, do quickly."

Judas had his feet washed. He ate the bread. He drank from the cup. Then he left to go make his deal with the chief priests.

And Jesus loved him.

Follow

A Prayer for Wednesday in Holy Week:
Lord God, whose blessed Son our Savior gave his body to be whipped and his face to be spit upon: Give us grace to accept joyfully the sufferings of the present time, confident of the glory that shall be revealed; through Jesus Christ your Son our Lord, who lives and reigns with you and the Holy Spirit, one God, for ever and ever. Amen.

Day 38

Maundy Thursday

"When Jesus wanted to give his followers—then and now—a way of understanding what was about to happen to him, he didn't teach them a theory...He gave them an act to perform. Specifically, he gave them a meal to share."[53]
—N.T. Wright

The Passover meal that Jesus shared with his disciples on their last night together was full–as it always had been–of powerful, intentional reminders about their *past*. It took them back to when their ancestors had been slaves for centuries in Egypt, and then God had miraculously delivered them from their oppression as they began a long journey toward the Promised Land. Really, it was more than a way of bringing the old stories to mind. It was a way of participating in the story, a way of realizing, "We are the people who were brought out of slavery into freedom."

As well as looking to the past, their Passover meal also always helped them to look to the *future* in hope. Just as their ancestors had been, they had also been under oppression for centuries, and they needed God's deliverance anew. Their scriptures pointed toward someone through whom God would accomplish this, an anointed one (Messiah/Christ), through whom their oppressors would once more be defeated and the promised freedom would again come–this time, forever.

Follow

By the time that they came to the night of that Passover meal together in an upper room, Jesus' followers had come to believe that he, their Rabbi, who was leading them through the rituals of the meal was the one through whom these things would happen, though they hadn't understood many of the things he had tried to teach them. Much that had happened in the preceding days was strange to them, but they understood what the Passover meal meant. They all knew the meal's rituals well, as they had participated in them in the same way every year of their lives.

At least, they understood the meal until–at some point in the evening–Jesus changed the ritual. "Take, eat. This is my body....Drink from this cup, all of you. It is my blood...." Jesus took this meal about their past and their future and pointed it–in their *present* moment–to himself, to his own body and blood. "Do this in remembrance of me..."[54]

John's account of that meal is very different, though no less memorable. In John's story, nothing is said about Jesus identifying the bread as his body, nor of the wine as his blood. Instead, John is the only one of the gospel writers to focus on something else that happened during the meal:

Jesus knew that the Father had put all things under his power, and that he had come from God and was returning to God; so he got up from the meal, took off his outer clothing, and wrapped a towel around his waist. After that, he poured water into a basin and began to wash his disciples' feet, drying them with the towel that was wrapped around him.

Day 38: Maundy Thursday

...When he had finished washing their feet, he put on his clothes and returned to his place. "Do you understand what I have done for you?" he asked them. "You call me 'Teacher' and 'Lord,' and rightly so, for that is what I am. Now that I, your Lord and Teacher, have washed your feet, you also should wash one another's feet. I have set you an example that you should do as I have done for you. Very truly I tell you, no servant is greater than his master, nor is a messenger greater than the one who sent him. Now that you know these things, you will be blessed if you do them.
(John 13:3-5, 12-17, NIV)

This provided the setting for the rest of the evening, in which Jesus gave his "farewell address" to his friends (though it was really more of a conversation), important enough that John devoted about 1/5 of his entire story to the dialogue (see John chapters 13 through 17). On that night which he wanted his friends to remember for the remainder of their lives, Jesus reiterated something to them no fewer than three times:

A new command I give you: Love one another. As I have loved you, so you must love one another...
My command is this: Love each other as I have loved you...
This is my command: Love each other.[55]

One meal, with two different accounts which each have an associated command: "Do this in remembrance of me" and "Love each other." These are the reasons this day in Holy Week uses the term "Maundy." The meaning would be clearer to us today if we called it "Mandate Thursday," as the root of these words, maundy and mandate, means "command." So this is "New

Commandment Thursday" when we commemorate, "Do this in remembrance of me" and "Love each other."

Just as the original night looked to the past and the future with a whole new meaning given in the present for the first disciples, it does the same for us. I hope that you are able to celebrate Holy Communion today with other followers of the Messiah, because when we do so:

- We are taken backward in time–back to that upper room with the astonished disciples when Jesus took the meaning of the ancient Passover onto himself. Each time we share the Jesus-meal, we again put ourselves into the old story of the people who are in bondage and desperately need God's deliverance. As the liturgy says, "On the night in which he gave himself up for us, he took bread…he took the cup…"[56]
- We are taken forward in time–the only thing Jesus describes as something that will be done in the age to come–after all things are made new–is to share in this meal again: "I tell you, I will not drink from this fruit of the vine from now on until that day when I drink it new with you in my Father's kingdom."[57] Each time we share the Jesus-meal, we are getting a foretaste of that final/first banquet with Jesus himself. As the liturgy says, "By your Spirit make us one with Christ, one with each other, and one in ministry to all the world, until Christ comes in final victory and we feast at his heavenly banquet."[58]
- We experience the wonder of what happens in those moments when we take the bread and cup together as Jesus instructed. He, the crucified and risen King, *is with us*, and his grace enables us to live more fully in him–and he in us. As the liturgy says, "Pour out your Holy Spirit on us gathered here, and on these gifts of

bread and wine. Make them be for us the body and blood of Christ, that we may be for the world the body of Christ, redeemed by his blood."[59]

As Jesus undoubtedly knew was true of his first disciples on that night, we too need to be strengthened by this meal if we are to be able to continue following him through the rest of tonight and into tomorrow.

Then Jesus went with his disciples to a place called Gethsemane…

While he was still speaking, Judas, one of the Twelve, arrived. With him was a large crowd armed with swords and clubs, sent from the chief priests and the elders of the people. Now the betrayer had arranged a signal with them: "The one I kiss is the man; arrest him." Going at once to Jesus, Judas said, "Greetings, Rabbi!" and kissed him.

Jesus replied, "Do what you came for, friend."

Then the men stepped forward, seized Jesus and arrested him.
(Matthew 26:36,47-50, NIV)

A Prayer for Maundy Thursday:
Almighty Father, whose dear Son, on the night before he suffered, instituted the Sacrament of his Body and Blood: Mercifully grant that we may receive it thankfully in remembrance of Jesus Christ our Lord, who in these holy mysteries gives us a pledge of eternal life; and who now lives and reigns with you and the Holy Spirit, one God, for ever and ever. Amen.

Day 39

Good Friday

I always underestimate how quickly this part of the story happened. If we read yesterday's and today's stories in the Bible, they take up a lot of space. For example, of the twenty-one chapters in John, one-third of them (chapters thirteen through nineteen) are filled with the content of these twenty-four hours.

This makes the pace seem slower when reading the story, as we read about Jesus getting passed back and forth between people, Pilate trying to figure out what to do with him, and the religious leaders working the political system to get their desired result ("You are no friend of Caesar....We have no king but Caesar."). Yet despite the change in pace of the narrative, the reality is that Thursday evening Jesus was having dinner with his friends–including Judas. By mid-afternoon on Friday both Judas and Jesus were dead.

As I've tried to let these stories sink in and picture the scenes of the Last Supper, Jesus' trial with the Sanhedrin, Peter's denial, the crowd's choice of Barabbas and insistence on Jesus' death, I've realized something: If I had been there and been a character in the story, or even just a face in the crowd, it's silly to think that I would have done anything differently from what everyone else did. I too would have been on the wrong side of the story and left Jesus alone.

I might have been one of those who loved Jesus but for various reasons couldn't do anything about what was happening, and therefore had to let it happen. Those such as Mary his mother, Mary Magdalene, John, Joseph of Arimathea, or Nicodemus surely hated what they saw happening but felt some inevitable sense of resignation to the way things were playing out so quickly.

Or I might have been someone who more actively turned my back and ran from Jesus, like most of his friends. I may have even reacted as Peter did and tried to cover up any tracks that I'd had with him. Based on my own history in circumstances much less intense than what Peter faced that night, I don't have much reason to think I would do any better than he did.

Or I might have been Judas. It's easy to believe that I could have been more interested in my own plan than Jesus' way. Like Judas, I too have been disappointed with God at times, feeling that he didn't come through as he should have, so who's to say that I wouldn't have been the one to seek personal gain as a result of Jesus not turning out to be and do what I had hoped?

Regardless of what role I would have played, I would have been among those included in Jesus' statement, "you all will leave me alone. Yet I am not alone, for my Father is with me."

I would have been somewhere on the wrong side of this horrible drama. And Jesus would have known that, and even in his most agonizing hours which I helped to bring about, he would have loved me anyway.

Follow

A Prayer for Good Friday:

Almighty God, we pray you graciously to behold this your family, for whom our Lord Jesus Christ was willing to be betrayed, and given into the hands of sinners, and to suffer death upon the cross; who now lives and reigns with you and the Holy Spirit, one God, for ever and ever. Amen.

Day 40

Saturday in Holy Week

Most of us have had moments of intense grief at some point in life, or–if we have not–we will eventually. My dad was my hero, and when we learned that he had terminal cancer, I felt completely unable to function. Much of what my life had always been was being lost. In the days following his diagnosis, I lived with a constant sense of having been kicked in the stomach, and I remember for several days waking from sleep, each time hoping that it had all been a bad dream. It always only took a moment for the dark reality to set in.

Matthew, Mark, Luke, and John each tell the story of Jesus' burial, but none of them say anything about what the disciples were doing on Saturday. There are some obvious possible explanations: it was a Sabbath, so they couldn't do anything actively. Also, since Jesus had essentially been executed for treason ("If you let this man live, you are no friend of Caesar."...Above his head they placed the written charge against him: This is Jesus, the King of the Jews"), the disciples must have been fearfully aware of the possibility that they would become the next targets. So, though we aren't told what they did, we can be reasonably sure that they hid, full of shock, fear, and grief.

Though my grief over my dad was intense, I'm sure it wasn't in the same category as what Jesus' friends experienced on the day after his crucifixion. In addition to the loss of their beloved leader, they also had to deal with the injustice involved, the devastation of their dreams and hopes about who they thought Jesus was (in their framework, a crucified Messiah was a contradiction in terms), the fear that they would be next, and perhaps most painful of all–the shame for having deserted him at his arrest.

If they slept at all, they surely awoke on Saturday hoping for an instant that it had all been a nightmare and that Jesus was still there next to them. After a moment, when the dark reality set in again, it is certain to have felt overpowering. Jesus' body lay dead and lifeless in a tomb.

The only detail the gospels give us about Saturday is one that reiterates the point:

The next day, the one after Preparation Day, the chief priests and the Pharisees went to Pilate. "Sir," they said, "we remember that while he was still alive that deceiver said, 'After three days I will rise again.' So give the order for the tomb to be made secure until the third day. Otherwise, his disciples may come and steal the body and tell the people that he has been raised from the dead. This last deception will be worse than the first."

"Take a guard," Pilate answered. "Go, make the tomb as secure as you know how." So they went and made the tomb secure by putting a seal on the stone and posting the guard.
(Matthew 27:62-66, NIV)

Day 40: Saturday

A Prayer for Saturday in Holy Week:

O God, Creator of heaven and earth: Grant that, as the crucified body of your dear Son was laid in the tomb and rested on this holy Sabbath, so we may await with him the coming of the third day, and rise with him to newness of life; who now lives and reigns with you and the Holy Spirit, one God, for ever and ever. Amen.

Easter Sunday

Because of the Resurrection...

Because of the resurrection…
Death is defeated.
Death itself is abolished.
Its sting is gone, because life does not end in a grave.
Death's primary expression, sin, is no longer our master.
> We can choose to remain slaves if we like, but a new, indestructible, full life-as-it-was-meant-to-be has become available to us.

Jesus' primary expressions, love and grace, matter more than death and sin.
> They always will.

Every opportunity to love someone and extend God's grace is an opportunity to do something that will last.
> Love and grace count more than we realize.

Great news!
> Suffering has no final word about anything. Jesus' suffering did not get the last word on his life, neither will ours.
>
> When it comes, suffering either shapes us to be more like our crucified and risen King, or–if we forget how he suffered before rising–to harden our hearts against him.

Easter Sunday

In Christ, every loved one who is no longer here is well and cared for.

We don't have to accept the fairy tale pictures of heaven.
> We too easily settle for thinking that we'll grow wings, sit on clouds and play on harps in a never-ending church service (does anyone really want to sign up for that?).
>
> Instead, God will make all things new–new heavens, new earth, new bodies…new creation, far better than any fairy tale we could imagine!

Jesus' friends expected that all of God's people would be raised at some point in the future.
> They didn't expect that point in the future to break into the present by happening to him on the third day after being crucified.
>
> Therefore, while we anticipate the future day when resurrection happens to all of us, the living Jesus enables us to practice his kind of life now, getting a foretaste of what's to come.
>
> We eagerly await the day when we and all those whom we now miss will be given new, death-defeating bodies like that of our King.

Thanks be to God! Eternal life is happening now, because of the resurrection.

Christ is risen!
Christ is risen indeed!
Alleluia!

Follow

A Prayer for Easter Sunday:
O God, who for our redemption gave your only-begotten Son to the death of the cross, and by his glorious resurrection delivered us from the power of our enemy: Grant us so to die daily to sin, that we may evermore live with him in the joy of his resurrection; through Jesus Christ your Son our Lord, who lives and reigns with you and the Holy Spirit, one God, now and for ever. Amen.

Notes

[1] The United Methodist Publishing House, *The United Methodist Hymnal* (Nashville: The United Methodist Publishing House, 1989), 353.

[2] The United Methodist Publishing House, *The United Methodist Book of Worship* (Nashville: The United Methodist Publishing House, 1992), 322.

[3] Ruth Haley Barton, "Practicing Lent: Invitation to Return to God," *The Transforming Center Blog,* February 21, 2012, http://www.transformingcenter.org/2012/02/2721/

[4] James Bryan Smith, *The Good and Beautiful God: Falling in Love with the God Jesus Knows* (Downers Grove, Ill: InterVarsity Press, 2009), 33-36.

[5] See Matthew 10:39, Matthew 16:25, Mark 8:35, Luke 14:26, Luke 17:33, and John 12:25.

[6] See Matthew 16:24, Mark 8:34, and Luke 14:27.

[7] Wesley says, "in every stage of the spiritual life, although there is a variety of particular hinderances of our attaining grace or growing therein, yet are all resolvable into these general ones, -- either we do not deny ourselves, or we do not take up our cross." See his Sermon 48, "Self-Denial."

[8] Mark 8:34-37, The Message

Follow

[9] N.T. Wright, *Mark for Everyone* (Louisville: Westminster John Knox Press, 2004), 111.
The idea of the political nature of the conversation between Jesus and his disciples that night came from Wright's commentary on this passage.

[10] "The Free Dictionary," accessed October 9, 2013, http://idioms.thefreedictionary.com/a+cross+to+bear.

[11] Gary Haugen, *Just Courage: God's Great Expedition for the Restless Christian* (Downers Grove, Ill.: InterVarsity Press, 2008), 113.

[12] Wright, *Mark for Everyone*, 112.

[13] These three areas are based on James Bryan Smith's "Triangle of Transformation" in *The Good and Beautiful God*, 21-31.

[14] Thank you, Robert Pelfrey.

[15] I'm basing this on the readings for Ash Wednesday from the Revised Common Lectionary.

[16] See www.daveramsey.com

[17] This study is known as "The Good Samaritan Experiment: Darley & Batton: 1973," description accessed November 5, 2013, http://socialpsychologyatpratt.blogspot.com/2011/10/good-samaritan-experiement-darley.html

[18] I explore these three ways of praying more fully in *Live Prayerfully: How Ordinary Lives Become Prayerful*.

[19] Adapted from *Live Prayerfully: How Ordinary Lives Become Prayerful,* Chapter One, "Praying With Other People's Words"

[20] At the time, this was the *Renovaré Spiritual Formation Bible*. It has since been renamed the *With-God Life Bible*, which is available with or without the "extra" books. It is an excellent resource.

21 As translated in *The Book of Common Prayer*.

22 Barton, *Invitation to Solitude and Silence: Experiencing God's Transforming Presence* (Downers Grove, Ill.: InterVarsity Press, 2004), 20.

23 Brennan Manning, *The Signature of Jesus* (Colorado Springs: Multnomah Books, 1996), 205.

24 Dallas Willard, *The Spirit of the Disciplines: Understanding How God Changes Lives* (New York: HarperCollins, 1988), 163.

25 Adapted from *Live Prayerfully*, Chapter Two, "Praying Without Words."

26 Adapted from *Live Prayerfully*, Chapter Three, "Praying With Your Own Words."

27 As quoted in John Ortberg, "'Tis the Season to Be Attentive," *Leadership Journal*, December 2010, http://www.christianitytoday.com/le/2010/december-online-only/tisseasonattentive.html

28 Richard J. Foster, *Celebration of Discipline: The Path to Spiritual Growth, Third Edition* (San Francisco: HarperCollins, 1998), 47.

29 Scot McKnight, *Fasting* (Nashville: Thomas Nelson, 2009), xxi.

30 Ibid. 81-82.

31 John Wesley, Sermon 27, "Upon Our Lord's Sermon on the Mount: Discourse Seven," in *The Sermons of John Wesley*, ed. Thomas Jackson, Wesley Center for Applied Theology, accessed October 11, 2013, http://wesley.nnu.edu/john-wesley/the-sermons-of-john-wesley-1872-edition/sermon-27-upon-our-lords-sermon-on-the-mount-discourse-seven/

32 See Steve Harper, "Week Five: Hunger for Righteousness," in *Devotional Life in the Wesleyan Tradition* (Nashville: Upper Room Books, 1995), 99-118.

[33] Paul Chilcote, *Praying in the Wesleyan Spirit: 52 Prayers for Today* (Nashville: Upper Room Books, 2001), 85-87.
I am grateful to Upper Room Books for granting permission to reprint this prayer in its entirety.

[34] The Apprentice Series is made up of three books by James Bryan Smith: *The Good and Beautiful God*, *The Good and Beautiful Life*, and *The Good and Beautiful Community*.

[35] Smith, *The Good and Beautiful Life: Putting on the Character of Christ* (Downers Grove, Ill: InterVarsity Press, 2009), 100-101.

[36] Willard, *Renovation of the Heart: Putting on the Character of Christ* (Colorado Springs: NavPress, 2002), 40-41.

[37] Ibid. 40-41.

[38] Ibid.

[39] Ibid. 95.

[40] Ibid.

[41] I don't believe this is an exact quote from Willard, though the idea of the process we are going through in life as shaping who we are becoming is central to all of his teaching. See especially Dallas Willard, "The Secret of the Easy Yoke" in *The Spirit of the Disciplines*, 1-10.

[42] Willard, *Renovation of the Heart*, 116.

[43] Willard, "Transforming the Will (Heart or Spirit) and Character" in *Renovation of the Heart*, 141-158.

[44] Willard, "The Secret of the Easy Yoke" in *The Spirit of the Disciplines*, 1-10.

[45] Willard, "The Human Body and Spiritual Growth," accessed October 13, 2013, http://dwillard.org/articles/artview.asp?artID=34

[46] Ibid.

[47] Wesley, Preface to "Hymns and Sacred Poems" (1739), as quoted in Paul Wesley Chilcote, *Recapturing the Wesleys' Vision: An Introduction to the Faith of John and Charles Wesley* (Downers Grove, Ill.: InterVarsity Press, 2004), 48.

[48] Wesley, Sermon 27, "Upon Our Lord's Sermon on the Mount: Discourse Four," in *The Sermons of John Wesley*, ed. Thomas Jackson, Wesley Center for Applied Theology, accessed October 13, 2013, http://wesley.nnu.edu/john-wesley/the-sermons-of-john-wesley-1872-edition/sermon-24-upon-our-lords-sermon-on-the-mount-discourse-four/

[49] Willard, *Renovation of the Heart*, 199.

[50] Willard, "Gray Matter and the Soul," accessed October 13, 2103 at http://www.dwillard.org/articles/artview.asp?artID=82

[51] Wesley, Sermon 27, "Upon Our Lord's Sermon on the Mount: Discourse Four," in *The Sermons of John Wesley*, ed. Thomas Jackson, Wesley Center for Applied Theology, accessed October 13, 2013, http://wesley.nnu.edu/john-wesley/the-sermons-of-john-wesley-1872-edition/sermon-24-upon-our-lords-sermon-on-the-mount-discourse-four/

[52] Wright, *Mark for Everyone*, 154-157.

[53] Wright, *Luke for Everyone* (Louisville: Westminster John Knox Press, 2004), 261-262.

[54] For more on the past/present/future aspects of Holy Communion, see N.T. Wright, *The Meal Jesus Gave Us* (Louisville: Westminster John Knox Press, 2002).

[55] See John 13:34, 15:12, and 15:17.

[56] *The United Methodist Hymnal*, 14.

[57] See Matthew 26:29.

[58] *The United Methodist Hymnal*, 14.

Follow

[59] Ibid.

www.ingramcontent.com/pod-product-compliance
Lightning Source LLC
Chambersburg PA
CBHW051651040426
42446CB00009B/1090